# FARMING CHURCH
## Cultivating Adaptive Change in Congregations

MARK E. TIDSWORTH

Copyright © 2017 Pinnacle Leadership Press

All rights reserved. No part of this publication may be reproduced, stored in a retrieval system or transmitted in any way by any means, electronic, mechanical, photocopy, recording or otherwise, without the prior permission of the author, except as provided by USA copyright law.

ISBN-10: 1548421804
ISBN-13: 978-1548421809

# CONTENTS

| | |
|---|---|
| Preface | 3 |
| The Readiness Indicator | 7 |
| Introduction | 9 |
| Adaptive Change Readiness | 19 |
| Adaptive Change Theory | 29 |
| Seven Key Cultivations for Cultivating Adaptive Congregations | 43 |
| Cultivating Faith | 45 |
| Cultivating Trust | 57 |
| Cultivating Vision | 69 |
| Cultivating Leadership | 85 |
| Cultivating Urgency | 105 |
| Cultivating Discovery | 127 |
| Cultivating Alignment | 137 |
| Start Farming | 147 |
| Appendix – The Readiness Indicator | 155 |
| Notes | 163 |
| A Message From the Author | 167 |

# FARMING CHURCH

# PREFACE

"Tell us the stories again."
Imagine you are enjoying a holiday with your immediate and extended family sometime in the future. This holiday gathering is beyond the time when the Church in North America has transitioned from church-as-we-have-known-it to church-as-it-is-becoming. We are on the other side of this major shift from the Modern to the Postmodern Era, having adapted to our new cultural context. Now, at this holiday gathering, those who are younger than you want to know how you accomplished the transition.

"Tell us the stories again of how you helped the Church move from what it was back in the day to this robust, life-giving faith community we get to experience now. Listening to you describe what church used to be like, it's clear church radically changed. How did you and your spiritual kin help this to happen? How did you work up the courage to confront your reality and make the necessary changes? How did you manage your grief while pursuing hopeful and creative new experiments? How hard was the journey? How did you keep going when you failed? How did you know you were making progress?"

Then you tell your stories. You describe the progress and setbacks, the forward movement and back-stepping, the joy and the pain. You tell about some who were lost along the way, abandoning their faith. You tell stories of so many others who were drawn into the Christian movement as it became more robust and invigorated. You find yourself tearing up as those memories come rushing to the surface. By now though, they are tears of joy, with the pain having washed away with time. Mostly, describing the journey fills you will a deep gratitude. Though the journey was like the Hebrews in the wilderness or the early Christians during the diaspora, you wouldn't trade it for the world. You are filled with an abiding joy.

One of them, after listening to the stories again, says, "Thank you. Thank you for being such a courageous agent of change. Thank you for shepherding the Church from what it was to what it is now. Thank you for helping the Church make those tough transitions so that we can now experience this. We are so grateful and blessed by your courageous effort. Thank you."

And you smile quietly, sharing a deep abiding internal joy with the Lord our God.

In 2015 I wrote *Shift: Three Big Moves For The 21st Century Church*, [1] ideal for those churches who are ready to adapt, moving forward in three life-giving, hope-filled ways. The conversations with clergy and congregations since have been fascinating. Many readily engage these shifts, using the content to move forward with direction and purpose. On the other hand, some clergy, church staff and congregational leaders have said, "I wish we were ready to shift, but we just aren't there." Continuing the conversation, it's become clear more cultivation work needs doing, increasing the readiness quotient for churches before they can adapt. For those who are ready to engage substantive change, *SHIFT* may be your launching pad. For the many other congregations who are ambivalent and hesitant around change, *Farming Church* is a more fitting place to explore your next step. Cultivating ourselves, readying ourselves to engage substantive change is where many congregations find themselves.

The purpose of *Farming Church* is to guide congregational leaders toward increasing readiness for change in their congregations. Over time, we've watched denominations and organizations roll out plans and programs promising congregational transformation. Unfortunately, so many of these fail due to the lack of preparation work before the new approach was introduced. Another way to say this is that when congregations are not sufficiently ready, their receptors remain closed when they are asked to receive new approaches. We need the eyes to see and the ears to hear in order to productively engage change efforts. We must be in a state of readiness in order to productively engage the mission-congruent changes before us.

This is why I've written *Farming Church*. With the time I have on this planet, I want to contribute to this Christian Movement in helpful, robust ways. No longer can we tinker with church, living as if being the church is a low-level, low-engagement endeavor. This world desperately needs God and God's Church. I want to be part of God's ongoing movement; God's world reclamation project (kingdom of God). So, let's partner together, applying our best leadership efforts to the calling before us, participating vigorously in Christ's kingdom.

FARMING CHURCH

# THE READINESS INDICATOR

How ready is your congregation for adaptive change? Later we will discover how readiness is the key which opens the door for congregational change. Given this, congregational leaders need effective tools for gauging readiness. We suggest the following three tools for assessing your congregation's readiness.

First, let's recognize and affirm that discernment around readiness can emerge from those highly involved, while also from observant outsiders. Those disciples who are very involved in the congregation may have a sense of the movement, flow, and obstacles within their congregation. Their high engagement positions them for discerning readiness. At the same time, their high involvement may blind them to accurately discerning readiness. Sometimes we are so immersed in the water, we can't recognize the tide. Regardless, those who are highly involved are valuable partners in discerning congregational readiness. But let's not ignore the valuable insights of observant outsiders. Through listening and observing closely, consultants, coaches, and clergy from elsewhere can recognize our readiness quotient. Their lack of personal involvement positions them to see the tide's rising or receding regarding readiness.

The second tool comes later in this book where we describe congregational readiness. Read the readiness indicators which are present in congregations who are ready for adaptive change. Compare these indicators with your congregation. Add prayer to this activity and you have an excellent collective discernment opportunity as congregational leaders.

The third tool at your fingertips is *The Readiness Indicator.* Found in the Appendix, *The Readiness Indicator* assesses your congregation's relationship to change. Seven Key Cultivations serve as the core of the *Farming Church* approach to readying a congregation for deep, adaptive change. The openness created through the interaction of these Seven Key Cultivations leads to congregational readiness. By completing *The Readiness Indicator* you will discover your change readiness overall, as well as in each of the Seven Key Cultivations. So before reading further, you are encouraged to complete the Readiness Indicator. Your scores will be referenced throughout *Farming Church*, becoming the foundation for your Farming Church Ministry Plan found in the last chapter.

After completion, we suggest your write your average score for each of the Seven Key Cultivations at the beginning of respective chapters. This will position you for reading with your particular congregation's current readiness level right before you. In addition, your Readiness Indicator scores can be combined with the other two tools noted before, leading to robust dialogue with congregational leaders. As you engage *The Readiness Indicator*, don't overthink it, but go with your first thought. Your first response to a question is typically more accurate than later impressions.

We decided to publish this Readiness Indicator within the body of this book so that readers have easy access to the Indicator itself, plus their results. Thank you for respecting the copyright of this published material, avoiding distributing *The Readiness* Indicator in other formats. We have considered publishing an online version, with increased ease of access and the ability to combine scores. If that format would be helpful and useful, please contact us so that we can consider developing an online version.

# INTRODUCTION

From the first brush with a congregation, it's already coming into focus. Every congregation postures itself toward life in some way. Some are leaning forward, engaging life as they find it, guided by hope. These churches anticipate good things, believing they are part of a life-giving movement. They live with openness, exercising an invitational attitude in relation to their community. They are caught up in the awareness that God is bringing the kingdom to earth as it is in heaven, delighted that God trusts them to contribute to this kingdom outbreak.

How do we recognize congregations who are leaning forward, living out their calling with vigorous engagement? What do they do that's different than others? It's not so much what they do as the attitude, spirit, energy behind what they do. When interacting with them, one finds a spirit of openness, engagement, liberty, life, and vigor. It's like they know something others don't. We find ourselves wanting them to reveal their secret; to describe what's driving their vibrancy. They go about their life as a faith community with confidence, knowing who they are. They don't engage in comparison thinking, wishing they were like other churches in their community. This results in a solid identity, with a flexible approach to mission and ministry. They are constantly adapting, engaging in constructive give and take with their community.

These churches are not defined by type. They are not constrained to one area on the theological spectrum, ranging from liberal to conservative. Their worship styles are all over the board. They are a part of every denomination and none at all. They do have theological viewpoints, do worship in certain ways, and are denominationally connected (or not), yet these indicators don't define who they are. There is something more, something deeper, which is the source of their vibrancy. They know who they are and whose they are; embracing their mission to be salt and light. They lean forward toward community engagement, adapting as needed to more clearly shine the light of Christ. When engaging these churches, one can sense their adaptive, proactive, life-giving spirit. Hope permeates their communal life. These churches are forward looking, eagerly embracing their calling.

But not every church is this way. Others are leaning back rather than forward. These churches are living as if the good news is not so good anymore. It's like the weight of the world has climbed onto their backs, slowing their progress to a snail's pace. Life for them is laborious, heavy, and discouraging. From the first contact onward, one can sense an ongoing low level despair. They appear to be like any other church, with similar ministry menus and organizational structures. Yet, something is missing. Due to many experiences and a long series of choices, they have turned away from hope, orienting toward despair. It's strange really…that people of the good news (gospel) could move to a place where it is anything but good news. These congregations also carry a disposition toward the world around them. They demonstrate a defensive, backward leaning, resistant posture. Suspicion permeates their communal life. Some of these churches are not so despairing, yet are neutral, bland, or lukewarm. Winsome is certainly not a word we would use to describe their current nature.

Most congregations live somewhere between these two churches. Most of us are a mixture of leaning forward and leaning back. Yet, taken as a whole, churches are either in reverse, neutral, or drive.

## Frustration Cultivates Change

There has to be a better way.

After ten years of church consulting, this was the new mantra playing in the back of my mind as I continued to work with churches on moving ahead in mission and ministry. There just has to be a better way. Our team at Pinnacle Leadership Associates was using a fine approach to visioning and strategic planning with congregations. Near the turn of this century, I learned our approach to church consulting, and visioning in particular, from a very reputable church consulting organization with a lengthy record of effective ministry. Early on, our approach produced great results, helping churches position themselves for forward movement. We regularly updated our process, adjusting it toward organic, communal, and spiritually-based work as we observed the changes in our culture which needed addressing.

Even so, we began to observe a change. The further we moved into this 21st century, the less effective our 20th century-formed process became. Diminishing returns was what we were seeing from our end of church consultations. We weren't hearing this from our clients, yet our observation was that the amount of effort, time, and resources going into the visioning processes exceeded the outcomes for churches. My frustration level with visioning work continued rising, indicating something was out of place.

So what was happening? Why were previously effective forward movement oriented processes growing less helpful and effective?

Change was the culprit. More specifically, the level of change was the problem. Though change has always been part of our lives, the speed of change in North America in the 21st century is exponential. During the 20th century we believed churches could make incremental changes, one step at a time, while remaining relevant. But with the dawn of this new millennium, levels of change needed by churches in order to be viable, relevant, invigorated communities of faith were rapidly escalating. The big picture explanation is that we are moving from the Modern Era (pre-2000AD) to the Postmodern Era (2000 and beyond), described more fully in *Shift: Three Big Moves For The 21st Century*

*Church.*[1] Without going into detail about this culture shift, we simply acknowledge every organization is responding in various ways to the large-scale shifts inherent in our new Postmodern world. As we went about consulting with churches, it became obvious that Modern Era-shaped approaches to church progress were declining in their effectiveness. Traditional and even somewhat innovative change processes typically do not include enough adaptive work to help churches shift into new paradigms. The level of adaptation needed exceeds the processes available for facilitating significant change.

In other words, there was a time in the recent past when experts could swoop into a church, recommending actions which basically improved the effort, commitment, and quality of what this church was already doing, resulting in productive activity. This was the Modern Era, when the church paradigm was fairly stable, with slight innovations (contemporary worship, seeker type churches). Experts could transfer best practices from one church context to another, helping churches improve their efforts, resulting in mission advancement. Then came the Postmodern Era, wherein most everything is changing. Now, so much has changed that the church paradigm we have successfully used is itself growing irrelevant. Now, we need new expressions of church in order to connect in meaningful ways with our North American culture. No longer does importing best practices from elsewhere improve our effectiveness much at all. Instead, the church model or paradigm itself must change. Tweaking our model simply contributes to more frustration and diminishing returns. We must adapt our church paradigm, moving from the church-as-we-have-known-it to the church-as-it-is-becoming.

In our high change context, it's fascinating to watch clergy, congregations, denominations, consultants, coaches, and everyone else interested in the Church, wrestle with this increasing need for adaptive change. The road to new effective processes for healthy change is never smooth. We are observing starts, stops, regression, and progress. Typically, we believe we can use the tried and true tools available to us (technical and administrative interventions) for initiating and implementing deep change in congregations. In actuality, those tools function themselves are part of congregational systems. Whatever we are currently doing is maintaining the church as it is. Simply ramping up our calls for culture change is insufficient when it comes to actual change. Well-intentioned church leaders are frustrated when their change efforts fail or produce minimal results. With brief investigation, we typically find the adaptive failure resulted from underestimating the magnitude of work involved in implementing systemic change in congregations. Not only is this true for congregational leaders, but also for leaders in general. John Kotter, a savvy change expert describes this well. *"A good rule of thumb in a major change effort: Never underestimate the magnitude of the forces that reinforce complacency and that help maintain the status quo."* [2] In fact, underestimating the work required to facilitate deep change is the most common mistake of pastoral and lay leaders when it comes to leading change. Given the times in which we live, we can now describe **underestimating the work required for adaptive change** as THE classic pastoral and lay leadership mistake of the 21st century thus far.

If underestimating the work of congregational change is the classic mistake when leading congregation's forward, then the **primary expression of this mistake is implementing change too soon.** Pastoral and lay leaders grow excited about something new, launching before the congregational system is prepared to engage this change. Over time, we've seen leaders launch change efforts too soon due to a wide variety of beliefs, perspectives, or practices (factors). These factors contribute to adaptive failure. Though they are painful to recognize, knowing them can save us much pain and suffering.

*Mistaking inspiration for timing*
Often leaders are visionary people who lead by inspiration. When they discover a new insight, a new opportunity, or a new direction for the church, they grow excited; ready to share this new discovery NOW. When they experience great inspiration through whatever means, they often assume this means it's time to begin the change process. These leaders must retrain themselves when it comes to large-scale adaptive change. Yes inspiration is very helpful when preparing sermons and needing an energy boost. At

the same time, because we are inspired does not mean the preparation work for change is complete or even begun. Leaders who recognize inspiration as a helpful tool, yet not a timing indicator, can use inspiration's energizing effect without undermining their change leadership effectiveness.

*Exaggerating trust levels in the congregation*
Isn't it ironic? Emotional intelligence research tells us that the higher one goes in an organization's hierarchy, the less accurate feedback one receives. This is especially true when seeking feedback about the effectiveness of one's leadership. [3] With minimal reflection, we can understand the influences behind this dynamic. Who wants to tell leaders they are less effective than they think themselves to be? We want to be team players, supporting our church. So we rarely tell leaders the truth. I remember one accomplished pastor commenting on this in a pastor cohort gathering. "As people leave the sanctuary and greet me at the door, I usually get two kinds of feedback. One is 'You are the best thing that ever happened to this church. You are single-handedly moving us forward.' The second is, 'You are the worst thing that ever happened to this church. You are single-handedly destroying the heart and soul of this congregation.' And I'm aware that neither one of those statements is likely true." This pastor was accurate in describing the challenge of receiving accurate feedback about one's leadership.

Here is where congregational leaders misread trust. Leaders typically exaggerate the level of trust in the congregation. After coaching so many clergy who believe they are highly trusted only to discover they are being asked to leave, overestimating trust seems to be the pattern. Lay leaders also tend to misjudge the trust they are given by the larger church. So, pastors and lay leaders initiate large-scale change, only to find they started without sufficient trust. We will explore what makes trust so necessary for leading adaptive change later.

*Neglecting Leadership Cadre Development*
What's your leadership archetype look like? All of us carry one, often so deeply ingrained in our minds and souls that it's hard to see. For those leaders coming of age any time before the turn of

this century, you will recognize the "strong man" theory of leadership (described further later). When he's needed, the strong man rises up and meets the challenge called for by the organization. Yes, when this leadership archetype developed the leader was typically male. Add the strong current of individualism running through American culture and we find ourselves believing we can lead change on our own. Female leaders are often not exposed to satisfying leadership models when the strong man leadership archetype is prominent.

As we will see later, it takes a coalition of congregational leaders to effectively lead significant change. Pastors and lay leaders who launch their change effort without a guiding and sustaining leadership coalition committed to seeing the changes through will not sustain the adaptive change process.

*Starting when urgency in the congregation is low*
Urgency is the motivation to tolerate the discomfort of giving up what's familiar in exchange for the possibility of experiencing something better, yet unfamiliar. When our motivation for change is low, the inertia created by familiarity wins every time. Congregations who adapt are driven by a high desire, or shall we say, **need** to become something more. When apathy permeates the congregation is not the time to initiate significant change. Instead, raising the urgency level precedes initiating significant change. Adaptive failure results when we believe initiating adaptive change will be the catalyst for raising motivation. Change efforts require the reverse, high levels of urgency to sustain us through the change process.

*Believing stating the case for change results in sufficient motivation for change*
Proclaimers (pastors and priests) are notorious when it comes to believing stating the case for change is sufficient. "If I can get that into a really good, meaningful sermon, then people will be on board." Or, perhaps you have seen it play out another way. "When we gather the necessary information; showing our thirty-year attendance patterns on a graph, then our congregation will be ready to change." There's enough truth in this factor to make it dangerous. We do need to understand why change is necessary.

Yet, understanding alone is helpful for only low-level minimal change.

*Underestimating resistance to deep change*
People change every day. We in congregations change every week. Much of the time we negotiate change fairly well, else we would be in conflict at all times. But when it comes to adaptive change, we meet resistance. Giving up something very important, like a spiritual ritual which was so life-giving at one time, is hard work. Our rhythms, norms, processes, and structures grow so familiar with time. We grow into believing our way of being church is not only one good way to be church, but the best or only way. In fact, we come to believe that being church the way we are church is what it looks like to be a faithful church. We mistake methodology for faith. So when we ask congregations to change, we are asking them to lay aside a way of being church which they have grown to cherish. Novice church leaders are often blindsided by the vigorous resistance to their well-intentioned recommended changes.

*Ignoring the obstacles and impediments in the way of change*
When it comes to congregational change, there are two strategies which bear good fruit. First, new experiences of faithfulness, growth, and engagement in the present can overcome obstacles and impediments to change. These new experiences lift disciples up into a new reality, influencing obstacles to shrink in importance. Second, some obstacles and impediments require direct attention. Time does heal some wounds, yet others fester without attention. The infection and toxicity in some wounds prevents healing until it's addressed.

When it comes to leading adaptive change, leaders must work to remove enough impediments for the congregation to move ahead. At times this means pulling off the scab, examining the injury, and surgically removing infection. We will need every resource we can muster while engaging significant change. Adaptive failure is highly likely when enough of these impediments and obstacles are ignored.

Since the classic adaptive change leadership mistake is

underestimating the magnitude of change before us, demonstrated by initiating change too soon, then what are we to do? Nearly all of our experiences with change processes these first seventeen years into this 21$^{st}$ century are screaming one word loud and clear – READINESS.

FARMING CHURCH

# ADAPTIVE CHANGE READINESS

Way back in 1995, change guru John Kotter recognized the need for readiness before launching change efforts, providing us with this challenging yet helpful insight:

> *"Until three-quarters of your formal and informal leadership cadre is 'honestly convinced that business-as-usual is totally unacceptable,' your organization's concerted effort to change is not ready to be launched."*[1]

Really? Three-quarters of the leadership cadre? Does he realize how much cultivation work that would take to get 75% of our congregational leaders to the point where they believe we must change? This was my first response after reading Kotter's insight. Initiating the change, jumping in and making it happen....these are what we really enjoy and believe to be the work of leadership. Yet, after moving through initial responses, we recognize the wisdom here. The title of Kotter's article is *"Why Transformation Efforts Fail."* So sure, we can move ahead initiating a change process without cultivating the growing environment...watching it fail. Because we tend to underestimate the work of adaptive change, we launch change processes before cultivating sufficient readiness in the congregation. Adaptive failure predictably results.

Growing aware of the complexity of leading adaptive change, I began to hear the failure stories while listening to congregations and their leaders. Too frequently there are stories of change processes which begin with great enthusiasm and hope. Yet, after a brief period (one or two years at most) of progress, these change efforts fade away. The congregation is left with low level disappointment along with reluctance to try anything resembling that experience again.

This led me to a working hypothesis. I've been observing congregational process, testing this hypothesis against the movement and experience of congregations. Now I've come to believe there is more truth than hypothesis in this insight.

**Seventy-five percent of the work leading to successful adaptive change in congregations occurs before launching the change process.**

Cultivating the congregational environment, readying the congregation for deep change, is the primary work of adaptive leadership. Long before the congregation engages visioning, or planning, or change, readying the congregation for change is pivotal. Without this cultivation work, the change itself is likely to wither on the vine. Pastoral and lay leaders are tasked with cultivating, nurturing, encouraging, and otherwise preparing the way for change. This means the vast majority of pastoral and lay leadership work is cultivation, readying the congregation for change.

One season in my vocational journey included working as a therapist, mostly with couples, doing marital therapy. Engaging couples around the dynamics at play in their relationship was invigorating and challenging. Over time, I grew very curious about one particular dynamic in the therapy office. After seeing couple after couple who were in relational binds and conflicts with each other, I began to notice that the couples who improved versus those who did not were much more alike than different. Their communication skills, conflict resolution skills, and desire to repair their relationships were very similar. What differentiated between couples who improved and those who did not?

In this context, I discovered a well-researched approach which became extremely helpful in my work. John Gottman and his research team at the Relationship Research Institute in Seattle discovered excellent insights which are raising the effectiveness of couples therapists around the world. Gottman and team discovered the 5:1 ratio. The principle below the 5:1 ratio is that what couples are doing when they are not in a conflict is far more important than the conflict itself. In fact, Gottman and team could predict which couples would enjoy happy and lengthy marriages by observing what the couples were doing when not in conflict. The 5:1 ratio is short-hand for saying those couples who contribute 5 positives to every 1 negative interaction will do well. In other words, the couples who do well are cultivating their relationship, investing in one another, when they are not in conflict. So when a conflict does occur, the relational hit is not so severe, with a speedy recovery following. There are so many more helpful insights in Gottman's work about relationship which will help anyone in leadership. [2]

Here is the takeaway for congregational leaders: The majority of the work when it comes to leading change is what leaders are doing before the change is introduced. **In fact 75% of leading change is cultivating the growing environment, preparing the congregation for engaging change.**

I remember one conversation in particular with an excellent leader who understands the cultivation work needed before implementing change. This leader is the director of a faith-based non-profit organization with a long record of substantive ministry in its community. Over lunch we were discussing the upcoming board meeting wherein the decision about a significant change in their organization would take place. Being curious, I asked how the vote might go. "O, it will be 7 for and 2 against," was the reply. "You sound so sure. How do you know?" This leader replied, "I never go into a board meeting wherein we are deciding on a major issue without knowing what the vote will be." Even more curious, I asked how this leader knows this. "We've been cultivating this issue for a long time. I've been in so many conversations with each board member about this that I've lost track of the number. Board meeting work is largely done long before our formal meeting." This leader, along with other board members, was cultivating change long before the decision to change was ever made.

So how do you feel about this readiness insight, about the fact that cultivating the growing environment is where most of our leadership effort is needed? This is not what many of us imagined the leadership part of our calling would look like. Leading change means implementing change in the minds of many clergy and lay leaders. We want to make change happen. Perhaps it's time to reframe our understanding of leadership, based on scripture, experience, research, and on the ground observation.

**Readiness Indicators**
Over time, farmers learn to recognize the readiness indicators for each part of the growth cycle. Is it time to plant yet? Farmers watch the weather patterns, test the soil's nutrient mix, and gather quality seed. The Farmers' Almanac even suggests the cycles of the moon are indicators of when the timing is right for planting.

Adaptive leaders are committed to cultivating growing environments, knowing this is the primary work of leadership in a high change environment. When readiness cultivation is successful, the result is a congregation who is leaning forward, ready to engage change with great hope for forward movement. Certainly we yearn to become these kinds of congregations, but how will we know when we are there? What are the readiness indicators in congregations when our cultivation work is done well?

*Most of the church moves forward with change rather than leaving, or threatening to do so*
Realistically, not everyone will go with us into the future. Some won't tolerate the growing pains inherent in adaptive change. Yet, when congregations grow ready for change, a culture of movement rises to the surface. When change is actually introduced, these congregations demonstrate a tendency to proceed, engaging the changes with hope. Their disposition or attitude toward change is friendly.

Change initiatives are actually approved through the church governance system. Not tabled, not studied forever, not processed so long they become irrelevant...congregations who are ready for change actually approve change initiatives. Sure they may discuss these changes with great feeling, yet they are willing to take fitting risks, approving change through their decision-making processes.

*Most of the congregation is willing to trust leadership when uncomfortable change is recommended and pursued*
We know a congregation is ready for change when they grant their leaders sufficient trust for leading change. Perhaps they are not 100% convinced this change is ideal, yet they go ahead and give their leaders the benefit of the doubt.

*The discomfort which comes from adaptive change is accepted as a normal part of church life*
"Over the next six months, many of us in this congregation will grow uncomfortable. And thanks be to God." This was the statement made in a sermon by a pastor of a church who was moving through adaptive change. The pastor went on to describe discomfort as natural and normal when a church is adapting. This discomfort was also framed as chosen. For the opportunity to participate with God's movement in their community, they were willing to persevere through this discomfort, knowing they would more fully live out their calling as a congregation.

How we interpret the meaning of change determines how we feel about change. Congregations are ready for change when they come to expect some level of discomfort is part of what it means to be church together. Since growth is part of the spiritual journey, we will experience growing pains. Ready congregations expect this dynamic in their collective spiritual experience. The discomfort inherent in stretching and growing is acceptable when we know it is part of our spiritual journey.

*There is an environment of holy restlessness*
There is an unpleasant kind of restlessness wherein we know something is out of place in a negative way. Conversely, there is a hopeful kind of restlessness wherein God is stirring us up,

readying us for life-giving change. Disciples in ready congregations regularly pursue living out their callings in new and richer ways. They are not satisfied with the status quo. Instead, they push each other to think outside their box; to consider new roads to travel. When they grow too settled, they grow restless, pacing back and forth until their energy is engaged in movement. Their restlessness is productive energy, inspired by God, and intentionally cultivated by congregational leaders.

*Excessive talk about the good old days decreases while conversation about the present and future increase*
We know congregations are ready to engage adaptive change when they are focused on the road ahead rather than fixated with the rearview mirror. There's an encouraging progression in their narrative when a congregation moves from nostalgia to readiness. In the nostalgic stage, references to what they used to do, who they used to be, and what role each disciple played in previous success are frequent. Literally, there are far more references to the past than to the future in their narrative. When congregations grow ready, the time-focus in their narrative shifts to the present and future. Their conversations are more forward than backward leaning. Yes, they take the DNA and positive themes from the past with them, yet they do not expect their future to look like their past. They are ready to engage healthy change. These congregations find themselves in a condition of readiness, leaning forward into the present and future.

Many of us yearn for this kind of church experience, invigorated congregations ready to engage life, God, faith, and movement. Aspects of becoming this kind of church are beyond our control, simply a gift from God. Largely though, this is the work to which God calls us when adaptive change is needed. Congregations become ready for change due to intentional cultivation of the growing environment by adaptive leaders.

**Farming Church**
Near us, right in the middle of suburbia USA, is a family owned farm. Forty years ago this farm was located way out in the country on a lovely, rolling landscape. Given its pleasant geography and proximity to town, subdivisions and new roads

grew up around this farm. Now it's like an agrarian oasis in the suburban landscape.

Each of our three children has worked on this farm when off from school in the summers. Their involvement has allowed a non-farmer like me to grow acquainted with farming life. I'm amazed by how many varied tasks go into cultivating the growing environment. This farming family is always busy, engaging in some activity which ultimately contributes to the likelihood of a good harvest. Clearly farming is a year-round cultivation process, much as it has been since the time of Jesus.

As recorded in the gospels, Jesus was fond of describing the kingdom of God with agrarian-based analogies. As he travelled across the countryside, from village to village, he encountered people who lived close to the land. They understood truths and insights drawn from their everyday experiences of farming. In Mark's gospel Jesus describes the growing process.

> *"The kingdom of God is as if someone would scatter seed on the ground, and would sleep and rise night and day, and the seed would sprout and grow, he does not know how. The earth produces of itself, first the stalk, then the head, then the full grain in the head. But when the grain is ripe, at once he goes in with his sickle, because the harvest has come."*
>
> Mark 4:26-29, NRSV

Mark's gospel contains some parables and stories not found in the others, though Mark was written first. This parable is different than many others, describing the growing process. I don't remember encountering many sermons or Bible studies on this parable. It's more a description of how growth occurs, rather than a call to action for us disciples. Yet, the insights embedded in this parable illustrate the nature of adaptive change. Let's harvest them, informing our cultivation work.

*Farmers cannot force growth*
Among the early disciples were zealots; disciples who believed violently overthrowing the Roman Empire would force God's

toward bringing the reign of God to earth (kingdom). Biblical scholar Henry Turlington describes this well. *"The kingdom is unlike the fanatical spirit of the Zealot. You cannot force the kingdom; you can only live according to its ways and share your understanding of God's rule. The final outcome is with God. His times and seasons are beyond us."* [3] This parable confronts the zealots, clearly communicating the kingdom of God comes in God's good time. Just like we cannot force plants to yield the harvest, we cannot force the kingdom of God to come in its fullness.

Adaptive leaders recognize that the kingdom of God has a life of its own. We are ultimately not in control of how much the kingdom is actualized in this world. Ever tried making a spiritual experience happen? We cannot "work up" authentic, genuine encounters with God. Instead, God gives these holy interaction experiences in God's timing. The very same is true when it comes to actualizing the kingdom of God in this world through churches. We are not in charge of the growth which comes through participating in God's movement. There is a Lord of the Harvest; who is not us.

*Farmers' role in the growing process is to cultivate growing environments*
So instead of producing growth, farmers cultivate growing environments. We have a distinct and clear role, yet we don't directly produce change. Adaptive change comes when the environment is cultivated toward growth readiness. Even beyond our cultivation efforts, change has a life of its own. Farmers focus on what they can control; preparing and cultivating the growing environment. Not being a farmer myself, I'm at a loss when it comes to describing the varied and numerous tasks involved in preparing the growing environment. What little I know tells me this is more than a full time job. Farmers are working year round to prepare their farms for planting, growing and harvesting.

This is the vision we want adaptive leaders to catch – a vision for cultivating the growing environment. When the church is ready to engage adaptive change, great progress flows. When not enough cultivation is done to ready the congregational soil, the seed will lie fallow. The great majority of adaptive leaders' work takes place before particular changes are introduced. Positioning, cultivating, and preparing are the work of the adaptive leader.

*Farmers act on faith in the intrinsic growth impulse embedded in the seeds*
Ultimately, farming is a grand act of faith. Farmers make a living trusting in something they cannot control, the growth process. They can cultivate excellent growing environments, yet they cannot guarantee the seeds will grow into a fruitful harvest. Ultimately, the growth process has a life of its own. Farmers are people of great faith, believing in the promise of the natural world.

This too is the bottom-line for adaptive leaders – faith. Imagine the faith it takes to step back, recognizing and accepting that we are not directly in charge of our congregation's results. How much faith does it take to focus on the environment, the context in which growth can happen, rather than the change itself? How in the world do we manage to step back, tending to other duties, while the seed germinates and grows? Most leaders who are interested in adaptive change are not low-initiative people. They are ready to engage the process; initiating change. Christian mystic Henri Nouwen helps us along with a statement in a volume aptly named, *Seeds Of Hope*. *"People who wait have received a promise that allows them to wait. They have received something that is at work in them, like a seed that has started to grow. This is very important. We can only really wait if what we are waiting for has already begun for us. So waiting is never a movement from nothing to something. It is always a movement from something to something more."* [4]

Those who wait have received a promise which allows and empowers them to wait. Cultivating change in congregations is an act of faith. We believe in the gospel of Jesus Christ. We trust in the gospel's life-giving power. We believe God will bring mission-congruent change, remaining faithful with God's work in the change process. We have received a promise which allows us to wait.

By now, you can see why this farming analogy is so congruent with the work of cultivating adaptive change. Seventy-five percent of the work of leading change occurs before particular changes are even suggested. The condition of the growing environment is directly connected to the likelihood of the seed's growth. Congregational ecosystems which are ready for change are far more likely to engage and integrate mission-congruent changes. So let's embrace our roles in leading change in congregations, cultivating the growing environment, farming church.

# ADAPTIVE CHANGE THEORY

Every leader's efforts are guided by his/her change theory. Often these are not clearly delineated, articulated, or perhaps even conscious, yet they function as guidance systems for leading or facilitating change in churches. Every leader believes a set of principles related to the process of change. Most of us gather input for our change theories from a wide variety of sources: on-the-job leadership experiences, formal academic courses, continuing education events, books, articles, blogs, podcasts, webinars, etc. The ideas, concepts, and practices we gain from these sources congeal into our personalized change theories. Some leaders can articulate their viewpoint while others intuitively draw on their change theory when needed. Regardless, all leaders carry beliefs and perspectives which guide them when leading change.

As mentioned earlier, change theories from the 20$^{th}$ century typically encouraged incremental change, given organizational models and paradigms were more stable. But now that the paradigms themselves need changing, we need robust change theories which include the capacity for deep change.

Perhaps that's why this new theory of adaptive leadership arose when it did. In 1994, Ronald Heifitz of Harvard Business School published, *Leadership Without Easy Answers*, introducing the theory of adaptive leadership. [1] Later (2002) his colleague Marty Linsky joined him in publishing *Leadership On The Line*. [2] More recently (2009) another colleague, Alexander Grashow, joined these two, publishsing the textbook for adaptive leadership, *The Practice Of Adaptive Leadership.* [3]

Adaptive change theory is not focused on what to do (content), but rather on cultivating the change environment. Like many of us, these three consultants turned authors recognize the time for incremental change is in the rearview mirror. For organizations to be viable, growing, living organisms which remain relevant and productive, they must develop the capacity to adapt to their quickly changing contexts. So we do a good service to organizations when we help them develop their inner strength and capacity for changing, rather than guiding them into specific changes. In essence, adaptive leadership theory teaches us **how** to change rather than **what** to change.

One key concept in this adaptive change theory is the belief the most helpful changes we can make will rise up from the dynamic interaction within our organizational context. We might call this an organic change process. In the church world, we are far beyond the time when denominations can create programs which work well in their churches across the nation. Instead, denominations are encouraging particular congregations to discover their answers within their context. We no longer (if we ever did) live in a "one size fits all" world when it comes to being church. We are now in a far more locally grown organic environment.

This is the focus of adaptive change theory; helping organizations cultivate their growing environment, developing the capacity for contextually-driven change. Though adaptive change theory is not designed for churches in particular, we find it extremely helpful for understanding and applying change in congregations.

As we move along, Adaptive Leadership concepts and practices will be introduced as needed. Yet, before moving ahead, there are four key concepts of Adaptive Leadership which are foundational to Farming Church. By the way, Heifitz, Linskey, and Grashow provide an Adaptive Change Intensive each summer. Participants report coming away changed, due to the efficacy of this approach, plus the high intensity learning experience designed and implemented by these leaders. Readers might consider participating when ready for a challenging adaptive learning experience.

**Adaptation**
*"The actions involved in enabling an organism to thrive in a new or challenging environment. The adaptive process is both conservative and progressive in that it enables the living system to take the best from its traditions, identity, and history into the future."* [4]

When it comes to farming, the farmer does not take a preconceived paradigm for farming and impose it onto the growing environment. Instead the farmer learns from the growing environment, developing effective practices and approaches from this contextual learning. Farmers learn about the soil ingredient mix, the nuances of climate, the wisdom of those who are experienced with this particular context, etc. This is where farmers begin; with the growing environment. The context of the farm forms the approach to farming, not vice-versa.

One might think that once the farmer does the work of learning and forming a contextually-informed approach, then he/she uses this approach as it is forever. From the outside, it appears that the growing environment on a farm remains static over time, requiring very little in terms of adjusting farming techniques. A closer look disproves this assumption. When visit the family run farm near our home, we recognize that it's surrounded by development in the form of roads, subdivisions, high traffic, and convenience stores. These changes are shifting the variables in the growing environment. What does the farm do when their creek is rerouted upstream to make room for more houses? How does the farming family adapt when the highway splitting their property becomes too busy to cross during rush hours?
On a larger scale, as global warming progresses, some plants are no longer thriving in their typical growing environments, migrating further north (in this hemisphere). In addition to changes within the growing environment, the tools of the farming trade are constantly changing. Technological advances are equipping farmers to engage their environments on larger scales

with more foresight. Weather watching apps and websites are constantly improving, providing farmers with greater ability to manage their work.

Similarly, the growing environment of the church in North America is constantly changing. In fact, this Postmodern shift is a radical departure from the fairly constant growing environment we have known in the recent past. The church shaped culture which existed up until 2000AD is deconstructing as we speak (Christendom). It's like a large scale migration is in progress. [5] Imagine that the majority of the population surrounding your church campus who favorably regards the Christian Movement suddenly decides to migrate to another part of the world. They sell their homes, load moving trucks and shipping crates; moving away. Then others move in to resettle your community. These newer people are not from Christian majority cultures, knowing very little about the Christian Movement. They only know what they read and see in the news. Most of them are neutral regarding church, while others hold negative perceptions due to their media exposure.

While this is occurring, most churches continue to function with the same cultural assumptions guiding their communal life as before the migration occurred. They put on events designed to attract crowds. They believe they will engage their community through slick advertisements and attractive buildings. They assume many people are interested in becoming part of a church, when in reality, many people have no idea what church is about. The cultural assumptions during the age of Christendom are no longer at play in many communities in North America, though many churches find ways to keep their denial of this reality in place. There is a familiar story floating around in the church consultant world with a poignant climax: "If the 1950s ever return, your churches are uniquely poised to take advantage of it."[6]

This is where Adaptive Change Theory is so helpful to the Christian Movement. Now is the time to step back, taking a critical look at our traditions, identity, and history, conserving the life-giving strands of our DNA. Simultaneously, this is the ideal time to lay aside the baggage which holds us down and restricts the wild and free gospel from flourishing. The calling of our generation is to help the church adapt to the world as it is now. We are spiritual shepherds, guiding congregations from church-as-we-have-known-it into church-as-it-is-becoming. Given the creative life-giving nature of the one whom we follow, we certainly have the creative energy it takes to make such moves in our spiritual DNA.

Here we are simply describing adaptation. Throughout this book we will explore how looking at church through the adaptation lens leads us to employ this helpful concept. Adaptation itself includes many activities, like increasing adaptive capacity, providing adaptive leadership, engaging adaptive congregational work, identifying the adaptive challenges in our contexts, cultivating an adaptive culture, and even adaptive failure. Embracing this adaptation perspective about church process loosens the systemic soil in congregations.

## Adaptive Versus Technical Change

It was like the light bulb finally came on when I discovered this contrast between adaptive and technical change. Many people understand there are different levels and types of change at an intuitive level, but most of us need clear, comprehensible concepts to make sense of our unrefined intuition. Contrasting adaptive to technical change is one of the most helpful contributions to those involved with leading change in organizations, including the church. First, we need more working definitions.

> Technical Problems = *"Problems that can be diagnosed and solved, generally within a short time frame, by applying established know-how and procedures. Technical problems are amenable to authoritative expertise and management of routine processes."*

> Technical Work = *"Problem defining and problem solving that effectively mobilizes, coordinates, and applies currently sufficient expertise, processes, and cultural norms."*

> Adaptive Work = "*Holding people through a sustained period of disequilibrium during which they identify what cultural DNA to conserve and discard, and invent or discover the new cultural DNA that will enable them to thrive anew; i.e., the learning process through which people in a system achieve a successful adaptation.*"[7]

Technical problems are clearly identified and described, lending themselves to solutions from current operating procedures. These are problems we like to solve, since relatively simple fixes do the job. Minimal creativity is necessary when solving technical problems, as well as little learning or research time investment. We reach into our tried and true tool box, or call in an expert with a larger tool box than ours, accessing tools, processes, and actions proven effective for this kind of challenge. We use technical know-how to solve procedural and administrative problems.

In contrast, adaptive challenges and problems require more from us. Learning, creativity, shifting, and paradigm-change are the nature of adaptive change. The tools which were effective in the past for addressing problems are ineffective. The problem itself requires greater change than the tools designed for solving previous problems can address. Instead, adaptation is required.

Consider for a moment the merging of two congregations into one. Theoretically, many of us can see the benefits of merging for both congregations who face shaky futures on their own. When both congregations discern this may be God's calling for them, the result can be life-giving. Merging congregations then is an adaptive challenge, requiring adaptive solutions. Absorbing one family from a nearby church which is declining is one thing (technical change), but merging two church cultures will require deep change. Learning, letting go, taking on, leadership shifts, and creativity are involved in this merging endeavor. Don't go into those waters flippantly. Though there are technical changes included, we are talking significant and comprehensive adaptation here. That's what adaptive change is about. Simultaneously, most significant changes in organizations are a combination of technical and adaptive change. Reconsidering the previous church merger example, we can identify plenty of technical changes involved, like closing one bank account while opening another, changing Christian formation curriculum, combining stocks of hymnals, merging accounting systems, selling property while upgrading other property. We need people with sufficient skill in these and other areas to pull off a church merger. These are the technical aspects of change. Technical and adaptive change typically is required simultaneously, yet we often address challenges as if technical solutions are adequate.

Recently I learned how a previously large Baptist church in the Atlanta, Georgia area adapted to its current context. Over time, this church's participation levels declined significantly. They found themselves with a large church campus, yet a small worshipping congregation. After a series of technical fix moves (reducing the budget, laying off staff, etc.), they revised their self-perception. Rather than see their church campus as exclusively reserved for them, they expanded their thinking to see the church campus as a community asset. This revision equipped them to rent space on their campus to multiple non-profit organizations for at very reasonable rates, providing excellent space in which these organizations could remain, affording space in their expensive community. Over time, this church was able to cover their facilities costs through rent, using the financial resources generated by the congregation for personnel and ministry support.

I know of another church who was praying for children and youth to join them. This congregation included a handful of youth, along with their middle-aged parents, while most of the congregation was older. They missed having children among them, praying for families with children to come along and partner with them in congregational life. During their season of prayer, one couple began volunteering at a local group home. The children at this home were in transition between families. Some went on to foster care, while others were able to return to their original families. Over time, the children from the group home began attending worship. At one point, the director asked if the children could also attend Sunday School, to which the answer was, "of course." So, this congregation found itself with a large group of children ready and eager to participate. They were from different racial and ethnic backgrounds than most others in this congregation. Also, they were participating without parents attached. So the adaptive move for this congregation was to expand their understanding of what it means to "pray for children" to join them. God's answer to their prayer looked different than they expected, yet it was God's answer. So they adapted, expanding their perception of what the answer could be, adapting themselves so they could embrace and love those God sent to them for loving.

Here are a few more examples to help us differentiate between the types of change we are describing:

| Technical Change | Adaptive Change |
|---|---|
| **Changing time for Sunday School** | Moving Christian Formation to small groups who meet in homes |
| **Improving quality of hard copy newsletter** | Moving to electronic newsletters |
| **Resolving a conflict between two groups** | Recognizing and addressing a pattern of conflict when the church grows to a certain number of participants |

So why is this discussion about adaptive and technical change so important? A classic mistake when it comes to leading significant change is addressing adaptive problems as if they are technical problems. When leaders apply technical fixes to adaptive problems they find themselves frustrated and disappointed. The old saying, "rearranging the chairs on the Titanic," shines the light on the difference. We may apply current know-how to a current problem, discovering this approach does not move us ahead. Larger, more expansive and significant solutions are required for adaptive problems.

When congregational leaders can differentiate between adaptive and technical problems, they are liberated to pursue helpful solutions. Congregational leaders who learn these concepts are able to more accurately understand the challenges before them. When a current problem or challenge is identified as requiring adaptive solutions, then leaders can step back and prepare themselves for deeper change. Contrastingly, when current problems are identified as technical in nature, leaders can avoid over-investing with time and energy, searching their toolboxes for appropriate tools or fixes.

**Holding Environment**
*"The cohesive properties of a relationship or social system that serve to keep people engaged with one another in spite of the divisive forces generated by adaptive work. May include, for example, bonds of affiliation and love; agreed-upon rules, procedures, and norms; shared purposes and common values; traditions, language, and rituals; familiarity with adaptive work; and trust in authority. Holding environments give a group identity and contain the conflict, chaos, and confusion often produced when struggling with complex problematic realities."* [8]

My first exposure to the holding environment came years ago in graduate school studying counseling theory. Later, while working as a therapist, it was clear to me that clients required sufficient structure around their personal work in order to make progress. Clients needed a sense of safety in the therapeutic relationship as well as in the literal physical setting of the therapy office. They needed boundaries around the counseling relationship, knowing they could relax into a safe environment to do their work without the fear of the therapist following them out the door. They needed an awareness of strict confidentiality in order to trust their secrets to another. Therapists work hard to build safety, security, and sufficient structure into the therapy process. This clear, firm structure empowers clients to move into the deep waters of personal development and growth.

Adaptive change theorists are fond of using the Pressure Cooker as an apt analogy for the holding environment as I described in a previous book. [9] Cooks who want to preserve vegetables for future use us the Pressure Cooker to transform vegetables from their raw state to a preserved condition. Transformational heat and high pressure are involved, making the canning process fairly risky when not done well. The Pressure Cooker is an apparatus which provides the structure and safety needed to contain this intense preservation process.

In similar ways, congregations need sufficient structure around them in order to engage the risky challenges of adaptive change. Adaptive Change Theory describes this kind of work as Adaptive Work. In order to adapt to new conditions successfully, churches enter a refining process, emerging from the pressure cooker different. Leading this kind of adaptive work requires sufficient safety, security, boundaries, and structure to contain the powerful energy of change. Churches who attempt adaptive change without a healthy and strong holding environment may blow the lid off (split or conflict) or not generate enough heat providing energy for change (apathy or spiritual depression).

This holding environment concept directly influences our efforts to lead adaptive change in congregations. Before adaptive change can be successfully engaged, sufficient strength in the system is necessary. The remainder of this book describes the seven cultivation practices necessary to strengthen the holding environment in churches, preparing and readying them for adaptive change. Here in *Farming Church* we will describe the holding environment as the growing environment. The congregational ecosystem is the holding environment, the focus of our adaptive change cultivation work.

### Productive Zone Of Disequilibrium
*"The optimal range of distress within which the urgency in the system motivates people to engage in adaptive work. If the level is too low, people will be inclined to complacently maintain their current way of working, but if it is too high, people are likely to be overwhelmed and may start to panic or engage in severe forms of work avoidance, like scapegoating or assassination."* [10]

Leadership is fascinating. There is science involved, but in its essence, leadership is more of an art form. There is not a manual, book, course, seminar, video which can give leaders the magic guidance for leading well in every situation. Instead, this is where the Holy Spirit intersects with congregational leadership. Leaders gather all their learning, intuition, discernment, and reliance on the Holy Spirit to lead effectively at any moment in time and as circumstances constantly shift and swirl. The Productive Zone Of Disequilibrium, a key concept of Adaptive Change Theory, heightens our awareness around leadership complexity.

As a congregation adapts to its changing environment, it is pushed, pulled, and stretched. Adaptive change is hard work, requiring us to engage at deep levels. So, there is danger on both edges while leading the change process. When we push too hard or try too much too fast, we may push the congregation toward exploding. We may heighten the pressure so much the lid blows off. The holding environment has a certain capacity. We may push too hard, exceeding the capacity of the system, leading to adaptive failure.

On the other hand, we may misjudge the adaptive capacity of this congregation, believing it to be weaker than it is. Then we do not push or challenge enough, lessening the pressures within the holding environment too much. The result is a low-energy congregation who is simply maintaining homeostasis without much forward progress.

This is the art of leadership – judging how much to turn the heat up or down. When leaders get it right, the church engages adaptive change well, resulting in new adventures and pilgrimages to new spiritual frontiers. Different churches have different points at which they are in the productive zone of disequilibrium. One cannot simply transfer programs, fixes, solutions, or other interventions from another church. There are too many contextual variables. What we are looking for is a productive zone, a place where the pushes and pulls between the key cultivations of adaptive change are just right, motivating healthy change. We want to be thrown off-kilter enough (disequilibrium) that we seek to right ourselves through adaptive changes.

## Summary

Taken together, one can see how congregational leaders who successfully lead significant change efforts intentionally and vigorously apply themselves to cultivating the growing environment. These leaders recognize we are asking disciples in congregations to function quite differently than their usual culture might suggest. Since this is the case, savvy congregational leaders recognize congregational cultivation work is a significant part of the congregational growth process. They know that no matter how appealing and attractive a particular change may be, it will be dead on arrival without readying the congregational growth environment for receiving and engaging this change.

On the first day of 2010, I began work as a part-time interim pastor with a very wounded congregation. They were well-known for their history of conflict, with the most recent conflict leading to congregational devastation. Part of their conflict became attached to the previous pastor, whose last act of defiance on his way out the door was to remove the over-sized pulpit, replacing it with a smaller, sleeker version. On the one hand this over-sized and outdated pulpit needed to go. The choir could not see half the congregation and vice versa due to its bulk. Worship leaders sensed this huge mass between them and the worshipping congregation. There's no doubt it needed to go. But, this pulpit was a holy artifact of this congregation, being hand-made by a former member. The congregational context was highly conflicted, not ready to even consider this significant change. On his way out the door, the pastor made this change without consulting anyone. No one was surprised at the pulpit's return the first Sunday after the pastor's departure. In no way was the congregational context ready for this change.

My one year interim agreement was insufficient for preparing for a new pastor. At the end of one year, I certainly would not recommend anyone who I liked and respected to apply for the position. The trust levels were still too low, not to mention the healing work yet undone. So, my position turned into a Renewal

Pastor Agreement, lasting three more years. Then this church was able, ready, and eager to call their next pastor, launching a good season of mission and ministry. About a year before the end of my call, we reintroduced the smaller pulpit idea again. We openly talked about the need for this change, facilitated discussions, and designed a trial period for experimenting. At the end of the trial period, only one person was interested in returning to the former pulpit. The end result was literally the same as what the former pastor had done; the smaller pulpit in place. But the reception to and embracing of this change was completely different. The difference was readiness. The congregational cultivation resulting in an improved attitude toward change, allowed for this previously highly charged emotional move to go smoothly.

Now, in our current high change environment, moving from the Modern to Postmodern expression of church, moving a pulpit seems like small stuff. The changes the Church is making now (those who will adapt and flourish anyway) involve deeper and more significant shifts. Thus, congregational leaders are called to make cultivating the congregational growth environment a high priority activity. Our aim is to lead our congregations in adaptive work which results in healthy adaptation; positioning them for embracing the gospel while expressing the good news in culturally relevant ways in their contexts. When we get a glimpse of this kind of adaptive growth, we find it extremely exciting. We start to resemble our spiritual ancestors on the Emmaus Road, finding our hearts burning within us.

## SEVEN KEY CULTIVATIONS FOR CULTIVATING ADAPTIVE CONGREGATIONS

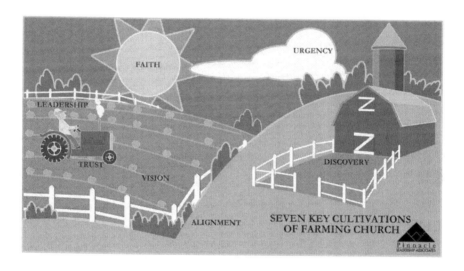

We were at the coffee shop discussing several topics, his church's progress being one of them. Pastor Scott described two clear, nearly simultaneous experiences which perfectly capture the congregation's posture toward change. Scott leads a church with a huge sanctuary, built back when large numbers worshipped there each Sunday. Now they are smaller, with these Summer months bringing even fewer to worship. In an effort to fill in the gaps in the sanctuary and create a sense of community, Scott roped off the back rows in each section while also closing the balcony. After the next Sunday, the congregational blow-back from a small loud group was strong. Statements like, "If those ropes don't go away, we are going to another church, and taking our offering with us," travelled along the congregational grapevine. This was the first of two simultaneous experiences. The second came the following Sunday in worship when the ushers who took up the offering were all female due to a special emphasis that day. The prayer before the offering in this congregation is led by an usher. Before praying, this particular usher praised this congregation for being open to doing things differently. She expressed great affirmation for a church who is willing to step out of its comfort zone, trying something new.

As Pastor Scott and I talked, we reflected on these two opposite experiences in the same congregation at the same time. We decided these two polar opposites describe the posture of we human beings toward change. We want to grow and change, yet we simultaneously resist change. We want our security and safety, yet we want risk and adventure. It's like we are inviting growth opportunities while also turning our backs on them. Mostly, we are ambivalent when engaging change. We are attracted and repelled at the same time.

This is the congregational context in which we are called to cultivate adaptive change. Congregational leaders must discern the fitting combination of pushes and pulls, of moving ahead and leaning back, which lead to adaptive change. The remainder of *Farming Church* is about those pushes and pulls. There are seven key cultivations which work together, readying a congregation. When each key cultivation is advanced sufficiently, then the congregational growing environment is positioned for adaptation. No one cultivation can stand alone, producing adaptive change. The energy for adaptive change emerges from the interaction of these key cultivations with each other. Our goal is to cultivate the growing environment so that readiness for change can emerge. This raises the readiness quotient, positioning the congregation for engaging adaptive change.

# CULTIVATING FAITH

*"Now faith is the assurance of things hoped for, the conviction of things not seen."*

Hebrews 11:1, NRSV

As human beings, we practice faith all the time. Even as I engage in the act of writing, I'm aware I've engaged in faith practice already. Before trusting my body to this chair, I placed my faith in this chair's reliability, believing it would hold my weight. Before applying light pressure to each key on this laptop, I placed my faith in this laptop's ability to capture my intention, translating each stroke into letters on this screen. As I write this, I'm thankful for the "save" feature on this computer, placing my faith in its ability to capture my words, preserving them in this manuscript. As I drink this flavorful coffee while writing, I believe I will experience the slight energy bump coming from the caffeine waiting for me in each sip. Evidently, we repeatedly practice faith every day.

Yet, as we read this famous faith description from Hebrews, we recognize there's a difference between trusting sensory confirmed objects (chairs, computers, coffee) versus that which we cannot confirm with our senses. When it comes to placing faith in God who is not seen, we are far beyond trusting ourselves to the observable reality of this world.

Before moving too far into this key cultivation, what do we mean by faith? One answer is to repeat the statement from Hebrews above. A central element in faith is mystery; not-knowing. For faith to be faith there must be something about it which is unobservable to the naked eye; something which requires a different kind of knowing. Sometimes faith describes a set of statements or beliefs about God (content). Other times faith is a word used to describe a group of people who share similar beliefs about God; the Christian Faith (descriptor). At its best perhaps, faith is the risky life-moves we make based on our understanding of God (action). Though we will discuss one aspect of faith as a set of beliefs about God in this chapter, most of our attention is focused on the act of faith. We are keenly interested in cultivating the faith of a congregation, cultivating our willingness to follow God into the mysterious future. We want to grow in faith; to become the kinds of disciples who do not need to know the destination before we launch the journey. We want to grow in faith, empowering us to engage God enthusiastically.

The longer I travel life's pathway, the more I grow to appreciate faith. I continue to learn that so much is uncertain and unscripted. God gives us far more freedom than we deserve, inviting us to co-create our lives with God. Minds with which to think, bodies with which to do, and hearts with which to feel are only some of God's good gifts to us. God trusts us to be good stewards of these gifts, granting us generous freedom to create lives worth living. Clearly, God believes in us far more than we believe in God.

Yet, even when our wills are aligned with God's will, there are no guarantees in life. We are called to do our best, and then trust that the best will work out. Certainly we each experience some level of pain and suffering, living in this fallen world. Simultaneously we will experience uncontainable joy and near-heaven experiences when following God's lead. So, each day presents a new opportunity to place our faith in God, to trust God with ultimate things. Though God is trustworthy, deserving our faith, we call it the Christian Faith, rather than the Christian Certainty. Our faith story, like so many world religions, requires its participants to trust in someone we cannot empirically verify. This is why we call it faith, rather than certainty. God calls us into mystery, into the deep waters of life with God, requiring faith rather than formulas. And, thanks be to God. At this point in life I'm so grateful humankind cannot reduce God to something our minds can contain. Fortunately, God will always exceed our full comprehension, requiring faith.

Farmers are people of great faith. Perhaps that's part of why Jesus was so fond of farming-oriented parables and analogies. Farming is one BIG LEAP of faith. On a recent trip to Wisconsin, I talked with Mark whose brother is a large-scale farmer. Mark described his brother's journey of inheriting the small family farm, later selling it to gain enough capital to invest in the large equipment needed to farm larger tracts. Now his brother leases thousands of acres, taking the risk of planting, cultivating, preparing, and harvesting each year. Much is riding on a successful harvest and steady market prices. "Just one of my brother's tractors costs more than the house where I live. Somehow he's able to manage the risk and keep things going." Every year Mark's brother places his faith in this large-scale farming operation, believing in its success, allowing him to service his equipment loans while making a profit. Though the farmers of Jesus' day did not risk on the same items, they certainly risked their livelihoods on the success of the harvest. Farmers engage a wild faith journey through their vocation.

Given the nature of faith and its central role in our spiritual journeys, cultivating faith in God is a key practice of God's Church. Before even considering change, we need an invigorated living faith in God.

Even when we are not considering change at all, faith is at the heart of being church. When our faith in God grows dry and brittle, this Christian journey becomes rote practice, religious duty, and heartless service. During these times there's little likelihood we will proactively and healthily engage adaptive change. On the other hand, when we our faith flows like springs of living water, we are far more likely to take the leap of faith adaptive change requires.

Discussing calling God's Church to cultivate faith seems so

ironic. Isn't it strange we need to call the Church toward faith over and over, again and again? In our humanity, we have a deep longing for certainty in life. So when we gather together in groups or communities, we collectively long for organizational certainty. We want to step out of our comfort zones, but only when we have the assurance this will result in the desired outcome. We are fine with taking steps of faith...when they lead to our preferred and expected outcomes. Of course designing and running our churches just like other organizations, using logic and human capacity as our priority guiding principles, negates the need for faith. When we run our churches as if we have no need for God's intervention or even assistance, we are idolizing certainty rather than prioritizing faith.

**Faith NOW**
Are there times in life when faith is needed more than others? There certainly are times when our faith is tested and stretched more than other times. Currently, the Church needs its faith on a grand scale. Only God knows if faith is needed more at this point in history than others, yet there are two major cultural dynamics currently challenging the Church, requiring great faith.

In recent presentations, I've found myself asking participants if they believe fear is greater or lesser in our society now than five years ago. Everyone describes our current culture as far more fear-based than before. We are constantly hearing leaders, newscasters, marketers, etc., tell us to be afraid. Yet, God's Church is perfectly positioned to demonstrate what it looks like to be a faith-based (rather than fear-based) community. If there is any organization, any group of people, any community in this world which should not be giving into the rampant fear in North America, it is God's Church.

The second current cultural dynamic challenging the Church which requires great faith is Christianity's transition from institution to movement. The following chart illustrates how Christianity is changing in North America; the United States and Canada in particular.

| **Christian Institution** | To | **Christian Movement** |
|---|---|---|
| Static, Stable Organization | To | Fluid, Changing Organization |
| Majority Religion | To | Minority Religion |
| Culturally Favored Religion | To | Culturally Suspect Religion |
| Cultural Insiders | To | Cultural Outsiders |
| Propositional Faith | To | Experiential Faith |
| Values Tradition | To | Values Innovation |

Since the last Great Awakening in the United States, Christianity has enjoyed many cultural privileges which come along with being the majority religion. Over time, Christianity developed sophisticated organizational systems (denominations), along with academically-based credentialing systems (seminaries). The role of Church and clergy in American society was front and center in many communities. Now, with the Modern to Postmodern shift occurring arounds us, the culture which supported stability for the Christian Church is deconstructing. As the Postmodern Era develops, Christianity is transforming into more of a movement rather than institution. Like the early days of our faith wherein the Way of Jesus was a movement rising up in the Middle East, now Christianity is becoming a fluid movement again in the West.

The response of Christian disciples and congregations is varied. Some are mired in the threat, loss, and grief which comes with change. Many others recognize this opportunity for reinvigoration, working to recapture the best of our heritage. This latter group of disciples and congregations are launching holy experiments leading to creative and innovative expressions of church.

To navigate these waters of rapid change, we need faith. Now is the time for God's Church to rise up and choose faith. Due to the darkness, fear, and mistrust in our society, we are standing on the threshold of one of history's greatest opportunities for the Church to be The Church. There comes a time when Christian disciples, as individuals and congregations, must decide whether to stake their lives on the gospel. How much do we actually believe the gospel? How much do we believe living in the Way of Jesus Christ is the world's best hope? It is time to lay aside spiritual malaise and fear, instead living with faith, hope, and love. This world needs people of faith, those who see a bright future due to faith in God. We are those who believe God is actively bringing the kingdom to earth, as it is in heaven. So, let's live what we believe, seizing this grand opportunity to partner with God to tilt this world toward the good. Perhaps it's time to integrate the Apostle Paul's faith further into our own. *"Now to him who by the power at work within us is able to accomplish abundantly far more than all we can ask or imagine, to him be glory in the church and in Christ Jesus to all generations, forever and ever. Amen."* (Ephesians 3:20-21)

Thanks be to God for this belief that God can do more with and through us than we think. This is the essential challenge of adaptive change...to rise up and become something which currently seems beyond our capacity. Congregations engaging adaptive change tread a thin line between invigorating challenge and overwhelming despair. They rightly discern they are being called to radical transformation, rather than incremental change. This is where significant, deep, robust faith is required.

Another way to describe faith is the fuel we need to empower us to step beyond our limitations, trusting God to empower us to engage the challenge of our times. We believe God will equip us for what God calls us to do. Faith pushes and pulls us beyond our comfort zones, giving us the courage to risk ourselves for the sake of the gospel.

### Key Practices For Cultivating Faith

*"Doing the same thing over and over, expecting different results."*

Definition of crazy<br>attributed to Albert Einstein

How ready are we for change? Inertia is that invisible, yet powerful, force which seems to pull us downward, making change difficult. Inertia whispers in our ears, telling us it's just fine to remain as we are. Inertia reminds us of all the good this church has done over the years; touching so many lives over time. Inertia tells us that changing now will only interrupt the good we have going.

Faith is the counter-voice to inertia. Faith whispers in our other ear, reminding us of God's hopes and dreams for this world. Faith also remembers the past, telling us about how our spiritual ancestors stepped out of their routines to live more like Jesus. Faith focuses our attention on God's power to grow, heal, and transform ourselves and others. Faith calls us to build on the good from the past toward something far greater than we can even imagine. So to cooperate with faith, to grow in faith, congregational leaders must cultivate our collective faith. These key practices are ways to focus our cultivation efforts.

*Preach and teach to the edge*
This key practice is particularly relevant to pastoral leaders, though many disciples are engaged in teaching in congregations. For those not personally involved in preaching or teach, the way you support this part of your congregation's life is influential. We all have a role in advancing the content of preaching and teaching.

What do we mean "the edge?" Faith itself is multi-faceted and difficult to describe. Is faith a substance which can be increased or decreased? Let's describe it that way for now, knowing faith is far more than this. Whatever level of faith we currently have is the level needed to support our congregation as it currently exists. In other words, we are seeing the results of our collective congregational faith. Then, when we are moving into a season of change, pursuing God's dream for us more vigorously, we need greater faith. Thus, we are eager to increase our faith. So then, is greater faith something we work up ourselves or a gift from God? Yes. Certainly God gives us the faith to believe, yet God also includes our volition and participation.

So, preaching and teaching to the edge includes discerning where the edges of our collective congregational faith may lie. We want to cross the proverbial Jordan River (faith boundary) toward the Promised Land (new faith territory). Pastors and teachers cultivate faith by holding up pictures of what it looks like to live in the Way of Jesus more fully. Pastors can do this through literal word pictures; or through all kinds of stories, videos, examples, interviews, articles, blogs, etc. The methodology for preaching and teaching this way is almost unlimited. The goal is to communicate in all possible forms and formats the call toward Jordan-crossing. We want to connect with the spiritual hunger of disciples in our congregations, inviting them to the faith-based frontiers beyond the edge of our current faith.

*Create safe spaces for engaging faith in community*
As we (Pinnacle Leadership Associates) engage disciples in congregations from various denominations, we frequently hear from them a desire for safe spaces within their faith community for discussing their faith journeys. It is quite ironic this faith-based organization (church) often is the last place we actually share our faith journeys. We hear disciples all the time yearning for the opportunity to engage real, substantive dialogue with peers who are also pursuing this life of faith. Strangely, many congregations are just not organized for this kind of significant faith-focused interaction.

Barna Research came out with research results in 2014 entitled, *Americans Divided On The Importance Of Church.* [1] This research clearly shows that Millennials are not so interested in church anymore, at least those raised in church. Here are some of the takeaways from this research:

- Only 2 in 10 Americans under 30 believe attending church is important or worthwhile (an all-time low)
- 59% of millennials raised in a church have dropped out
- 35% of millennials have an anti-church stance, believing church does more harm than good
- Millennials are the age group least likely to attend church (by far)

Millennials are not the only voice we need to hear, yet they are speaking for many when they describe the lack of opportunity to engage real life issues in helpful ways in congregations. When do we get to talk about our struggles to hold onto faith? Where can we engage the issues of our day as they intersect our faith? When will we develop enough maturity to share this level of spiritual engagement and remain in relationship? Too many people do not experience this in congregations so they write them off as irrelevant. They can have these conversations with friends at the pub or restaurant already.

Even so, many disciples hunger for these kinds of conversations in the context of church. This is why we are part of a congregation...to engage faith with a community of faith. So let's design ways to do this, gathering in groups for significant faith sharing, including highs and lows of this faith journey.

*Identify and cultivate the congregation's practical theology regarding change*
Later we will give significant attention to a congregation's posture toward change. That posture is an expression of the congregation's practical theology regarding change. By mentioning practical theology we are not suggesting cognitively based propositions about God. Instead we are talking about what we really believe when we are trying to make it through life. In the middle of the night, when we are afraid, what is it we know about God and God's ways with us which brings comfort to our souls? When our backs are against the wall with nowhere to turn, what do we know which allows us to persevere? When we are facing challenging circumstances, doubting we have the capacity to overcome and move through; what do we know then? These kinds of questions move us from theological propositions to actualized faith. So what do we know, deep down in our bones, about God when it comes to congregational change? Allow me to share some of what I've come to know.

- God provides what we need in order to do what God calls us to do
- We need not fear change in the present and future, since perfect love (God's love) casts out fear
- God's Church has reinvented itself over and over again throughout history
- God knows how to lead the Church through change

I could go on, yet these are enough examples to help you lead your congregation in this important faith-focused exercise. We can imagine disciples sitting around tables engaging this conversation. Or better yet, visualize laying out the invitation to identify one's practical theology, returning in a couple weeks to share what's discovered. Collecting these faith-statements, processing them as a group (congregation), helps us recognize our collective theology regarding change. This activity in itself cultivates our faith regarding congregational change.

*Challenge the congregation to attempt what's beyond current perceived capacity*
If God withdrew God's presence and power from our congregation for some strange reason, what would change? Would everything click along as usual? Better yet, how long would it take us to notice God's withdrawal in practical terms? If we would not immediately and desperately notice this, then we are not making room for God in our congregational life.

We can understand this spiritual dynamic in two ways, both valid. One, God has already given us many gifts for mission-congruent ministry. So, we believe God is active in everything we do as a congregation. Therefore, we do what we are able to do, giving God the glory for the gifts and capacity which allows us to do so. Two, God often provides what we need when we step into the void, when we attempt greater things for God.

This second way is what we are suggesting; attempting what's beyond our current perceived capacity. The congregation will need greater faith when the congregation is attempting that which they believe is beyond their native ability. Adopting a budget which requires more money than is pledged, trusting God to bring the increase, requires faith. Engaging our community to serve in greater ways than we believe we can requires faith.

Congregational leaders who challenge us to rise up beyond our perceived capacity cultivate faith among us. We find ourselves praying with statements like, "God, if you want this done, you are going to have to supply the strength and resources, because we don't have what it takes. Nevertheless, we are following your call to pursue this step of faith." Living by faith drives us to our knees, increasing our dependence on God.

Another way to cultivate faith which I'm not mentioning here is to encourage every disciple in the congregation to engage in spiritual disciplines. Right or wrong, I'm assuming congregational leaders are actively doing this already, not requiring prompting to do so.

# CULTIVATING TRUST

*"The best way to find out if you can trust somebody is to trust them."*

Ernest Hemingway

At this current point in history in North America, trust as an entity is struggling. As I write these words, the 2016 presidential election is recently completed. The primaries and then the campaign itself were bruising experiences for the United States. The extreme and harsh rhetoric of the candidates mirrored the significant divides in the electorate. The candidates themselves felt free to speak to and about each other with unprecedented harshness. Add to this the efforts of other countries to influence our elections and the trust levels for leadership decline even more. Postmodernism already brought a clear decline in trust for institutions, corporations, and organizations of all kinds. Now the political experience of many lowers trust even more. Americans are observing how a lack of trust for and among political leaders can slow the progress of an entire nation.

Even so, trust in congregations is even more important. When it comes to leading congregations effectively, sufficient trust is necessary. The last chapter described faith as the pathway to an invigorated relationship with God. Now we are turning our attention to the relationships among the disciples in a congregation. Faith involves ultimate concerns, directing our attention toward God. Trust describes a major dynamic in our relationships with each other. Trust is the currency congregational leaders spend when calling people to rise up and move to a new place. When we trust congregational leaders, we are more willing to travel to a land which we "know not of." When we trust our congregation's leadership, our willingness to risk, let go, and adapt increases. When trust is low in congregations, our willingness to step outside our comfort zones, quickly declines.

**How Much Trust Is Enough?**
Does the trust level in a congregation ever reach 100%? There is always a trust-deficit in any group of human beings, knowing even the best and most trustworthy among us, is flawed. God is completely trustworthy, though we are not. The very good news is that 100% trust is not required or expected. People realize that God deserves our ultimate faith, but we trust people incompletely. Given this, congregational leaders are looking for *sufficient* trust. We need enough trust to make decisions, engage change, and move forward. Trust is our working capital in congregations, without the need for our trust-funds to be fully stocked. So, how do we know when sufficient trust is present for leading adaptive change? How do we know when trust levels are sufficient to ready the congregation to engage adaptive its adaptive challenges?

*There is sufficient trust in the congregation when much of the congregation grants leaders the benefit of the doubt (BOD).* When congregations believe their leaders have good intentions in their hearts, trying to lead the church toward fulfilling its calling, then they are willing to grant sufficient trust to those leaders.

Recently I was with the lay leaders of a church who was experiencing conflict. The conflict was not rampant in the church, yet it was significant enough they called in a consultant to help. This was the initial meeting, designed for listening and learning their story. Before listening, typically I describe the assumptions I bring to the conflict management process. One assumption is the belief that every disciple involved loves God and wants good things for God's church. I assume the participants in this church are doing what they are doing (even if misguided) because they want their church to flourish. In response, one disciple noted they had drifted away from this assumption. They were allowing a cloud of suspicion to descend into their faith community, making it difficult to see the good intentions of each other through the suspicion mists. Trust levels in this church were very low, preventing much forward movement.

When trust levels are insufficient, disciples in congregations tend to deny trust to each other, thinking the worst when it comes to interpreting intentions. Consider the following list of negative assumptions disciples carry regarding others in the congregation when trust is insufficient. Rarely would one say these aloud, but often they are the internal commentary running in the background.

- "Your intention in this is to take something away from me."
- "Your intention in is to gain more control and influence for yourself, while lessening mine with the congregation."
- "You are trying to move your agenda forward; disregarding my agenda."
- "You are selfish, always wanting your way."
- "You are not open to influence or discussion; it's your way or the highway."
- "Your intention is to fight any suggestion I make, especially if it involves you giving, shifting, or changing."

But when trust levels are sufficient, the internal dialogue of assumptions changes. When engaging one another and observing the actions of others, disciples with sufficient trust give one another the BOD.

- "Your strong feelings about this are an indicator of how invested you are in this church."
- "You really want this church to be effective in accomplishing its mission."
- "Your human flaws will interfere with what we are doing here sometimes (as do mine), but that doesn't reflect what's in your heart nor your intentions."
- "Your passion for your point of view grows out of your deep love for God and for this church."

- "Your behavior, which I experienced as hurtful, doesn't necessarily mean you meant to hurt me."
- "You generally want us to succeed."

A strong indicator sufficient trust levels exist is when we practice granting the BOD to each other in congregations.

*There is sufficient trust in the congregation when effective working relationships are in place.* In most workplaces, we recognize the need for effective working relationships in order to achieve our purposes. Often the times when we grow aware of this reality is when working relationships are not in place. When too much tension lingers or unresolved conflict grows, then our productivity declines. This dynamic is alive and well in churches too. The working relationships at play between the pastor(s), staff, lay leadership team, committees, task forces, teams, and congregation directly influence trust levels. Investing in these relationships with an eye toward working well together, will raise trust levels in the congregation.

*There is sufficient trust for change in the congregation when disciples are willing to take risks on the recommendation of leaders.* Do we realize what we are really asking disciples in congregations to do? When leading adaptive change we are asking people to let go of cherished and familiar ways of being church in order to move to a new land they have not yet seen. Heifetz and Linsky describe this well, *"To persuade people to give up the love they know for a love they've never experienced means convincing them to take a leap of faith in themselves and in life."*[1]

Given the challenging nature of adaptive change, we must trust those leading us toward change in order to follow. When sufficient trust is present in the congregation, disciples will make statements like the following. "I'm not completely convinced this action is the best thing for us to do, but since you are recommending it, I will give it a try." Disciples in churches may step out in faith, taking risks, not because the particular change draws them forward, but because they trust their leaders. Since they trust their leadership sufficiently, they are willing to risk, despite their misgivings about the changes themselves.

## Key Practices For Cultivating Trust

Before we move too far into this key practice of cultivating trust, we must acknowledge the unusual nature of trust itself. Directly increasing trust is beyond our control, like directly producing growth is beyond the farmer's direct influence. Trust grows as a result of other actions whose purpose is not specifically to increase trust. In our farming analogy, cultivating trust is like cultivating the growing environment. We don't make growth occur. Instead, we cultivate the growing environment. The growth itself has a life of its own. Simultaneously we can cultivate the trust environment towards growth. Here is where the faith of leaders is needed. Our faith calls us to believe trust will develop when we cultivate the growing environment with intentionality. These key practices fertilize the growing environment, making it more likely that trust will grow.

Two primary factors which are less under our control, influence trust in congregations: time and experience. A certain level of trust is granted to pastoral and lay leaders simply because they are called to serve in their positions. Leaders enjoy some level of trust from the beginning. Yet, this small level of positional trust only allows us to walk through the leadership doorway. Leaders are equipped to lead very low level change with this beginning positional trust level. To lead adaptive change, time is required, cultivating sufficient trust for deep change. Experience is the other primary factor contributing to trust. When we experience a leader as trustworthy over time, then we build the experiential trust quotient, coming to see that leader as trustworthy.

The following actions synthesize together, reinforcing and interacting with each other, resulting in a relational field of sufficient trust. Though we can't create trust by focusing directly on it, trust does grow when we combine the following actions.

### *Practicing Faithfulness*
Many of us aspire to faithfulness, wanting to be able to look back toward the end of our life's journey and say we were faithful to our callings. Certainly we cannot say this with complete assurance, yet when it comes to fulfilling the major part of our callings, we want to be faithful. We aspire to faithfully love those

God gives us to love, serving well in God's vineyard.

When the congregation experiences its leaders as faithfully executing their callings, they trust them even more. This begins by doing what seems to be ordinary leadership activity. Consistently showing up; being physically, emotionally, and relationally present on a day to day basis, cultivates trust.

Faithfulness also applies to larger issues. How many stories do we know of charismatic pastoral leaders who convince congregations to take large risks (often in terms of buildings and mortgages) followed by leaving for easier pastoral assignments? These congregations are left with a sense of abandonment, given their trust in the pastoral leader to remain with them, seeing the challenge through. Faithfulness often means staying through the challenges, especially when they were taken on due to one's leadership.

This practice of being faithful gives us guidance when it comes to assessing the timing for adaptive change efforts. Most leaders know the two common approaches to change. One approach is to take advantage of the openness in the church when leaders are new, initiating change right away, making the most of the initial trust extended to leaders. The other approach is to listen and learn, followed by launching change efforts when the congregation develops trust through the demonstrated faithfulness of leaders. Since we are discussing trust in such depth, you may not be surprised to learn that adaptive change requires significant trust levels, necessitating sufficient time. Some congregational change experts, like Israel Galindo, recommend delaying visioning in congregations for at least five years after the new pastor arrives.[2] Though five years may seem extreme, the faithfulness of pastoral and lay leaders over time cultivates sufficient trust for the significant organizational risks involved in adaptive change.

*Practicing Integrity*
Though integrity may be faithfulness' relative, it's not the same. Faithfulness is more about fulfilling the duties and expectations of one's calling and position. Integrity is more about the person of the leader, how she goes about her leadership ministry.

Leaders with high integrity say what they mean and mean what they say. There is little daylight between their words and their actions. High integrity persons are integrated people, having made peace with their internal drives, exhibiting a congruence in who they are across many different public and private contexts.

I'm remembering one pastor who was extremely gifted in terms of persuading, communicating, and helping others feel good about themselves. His high energy and forward movement orientation drew the disciples in the congregation forward, leading to high level change. Unfortunately, this pastor also had the tendency to promise far more than could be delivered. His excitement about accomplishing the vision allowed his enthusiasm to outrun his judgement. The practical outcome of this dynamic was promises and assurances given to multiple groups and individuals which were not fulfilled. Over time, this pastor's ministry lost credibility as disciples in the congregation began to connect the dots by comparing stories. The trust level eventually dipped too low for productive ministry to proceed, requiring a pastoral move. Though it may be inconvenient at times, or lead to short-term disappointment, practicing integrity through congruent words and actions will cultivate trust.

*Serving Well*
There are two necessary components when it comes to serving well in congregations. Both pastoral and lay leaders need each, combining to empower effective leadership. Love for God and people is the first component. Love is the baseline competency for leaders in congregations. Do you remember how Jesus described leadership in the gospels? He demonstrated what it looks like to be a leader in this Christian community by taking on the role of a servant, washing the dirty feet of his disciples. Serving others through love…this is what Christian leadership looks like. So, congregational leaders must be disciples who love others. Without this basic quality and action, leaders will not be trusted. The old saying still provides very helpful wisdom for us, "They don't care how much you know until they know how much you care."
The second component of serving well in congregational leadership is competence. Every profession and job requires

people in positions to be competent in their craft. There is church-craft involved in pastoral and lay leadership. Pastors must be able to design meaningful worship experiences and deliver effective sermons. Lay leaders must understand their church's polity well enough to use the processes available to them as they lead. Pastors and lay leaders need a basic level of competence in their particular duties. When they demonstrate their competence, disciples in the congregation trust them more fully, believing these leaders are capable of leading them through change.

Before launching your adaptive change effort, first take the time to demonstrate your basic competence in what you are called to do. In addition, assess your leadership team, considering the competence of each person. We are not asking for perfection, or even exceptional leadership here. We are recognizing that basic competence in the functions of one's role provides the foundation for disciples to trust leaders with higher level change. When we know our leaders love the church and are basically competent in their roles, we grant them trust.

*Listening Deeply*
Who in our world actually listens to others? Certainly some professionals are paid to do so, but who in our daily lives listens to us? When we engage someone who listens deeply, we are surprised and pleased. Listening, it turns out, is a form of love. When leaders are able to set aside their agendas and listen, we recognize they care. Tuning into someone's experience, listening deeply, communicates love. When leaders listen, it's like they are saying, "I see you and recognize you are there. I want to know you and your point of view because you matter." We experience love when others listen deeply to our perspectives.

Leaders know they are listening well to the congregation when disciples start making statements like, "Our pastor gets us," or "Our Lay Leadership Team Chair understands where we are as a church." Then we know we are listening well enough to communicate back to the congregation where we perceive them to be in their journey as a church. When we listen deeply, something fascinating happens. When disciples in congregations know they are heard by leaders, they don't have to agree with everything leadership proposes in order to follow. When we know we are heard, we are far more cooperative. We don't insist on everything going our way when we know we count and are taken seriously. The listening and understanding done by leaders helps us to trust their leadership.

*Pursuing Small Wins*
There is that short, yet insightful statement in the gospel of Luke, *"Whoever is faithful in a very little is faithful also in much; and whoever is dishonest in a very little is dishonest also in much. If then you have not been faithful with the dishonest wealth, who will entrust to you the true riches?" (Luke 16:10-11)*

Perhaps this is how trust grows. When leaders are faithful with small level changes, then we trust them with larger level changes. Each successful experience of navigating change encourages us to trust these leaders when they suggest deeper change.

The first Sunday of an interim pastorate brought quite a surprise to me. I was sitting on the front row, ready to stand to deliver announcements, when the starting time for worship came and went. The choir had not yet processed into the choir loft and the musician was just beginning the prelude. At nearly ten minutes after the hour everyone was in place for worship to begin. I thought this odd, but gave the benefit of the doubt, since this was the first Sunday with this new interim pastor onboard. After the same experience repeated itself the following Sunday, I discussed this with the staff team, strategizing about making the small change to begin worship at the announced and expected time. The following Sunday worship began on time, as it continued to do thereafter. The response was far larger than expected. So many disciples in that congregation offered words of affirmation to the worship leaders for beginning on time. Evidently, ever since the worship leaders had slipped into the habit of starting whenever they were ready, many in that congregation found this disconcerting. The culture of that particular congregation and community valued beginning on time. This small change produced a larger "win" than anyone expected. Worship leaders gained credibility and trust through this small action.

In every congregation, there are ways leaders can help the congregation improve or change their way of being church which costs very little in effort and emotional energy. Through identifying the small win opportunities, enacting the needed changes, leaders build leadership capital in the form of trust.

*Taking Initiative*
Leaders who move ahead, exercising initiative often elicit trust from the congregation. We perceive these leaders as disciples who care enough to lean into their leadership roles. Their initiative demonstrates their heart's desire, helping this church move forward in mission and ministry. When leaders want to practice initiative in their leadership roles, there are two primary ways to channel this energy.

First, effective leaders take initiative toward the future. They anticipate what's coming; calling to attention actions or plans which will position the congregation for healthy engagement of the future. Sometimes this is as simple as effective calendar planning, organizing ourselves well for future action. A more sophisticated leadership initiative activity is anticipating future shifts which require larger changes from the church. Practicing initiative in smaller ways (like calendaring) will cultivate trust for taking initiative in larger ways.

Second, effective leaders take initiative to resolve concerns in the present, which may include lingering issues from the past. Relief…that's the typical response when leaders surface a conversation which needs to take place. Relief also happens when leaders take action to dismiss a staff member who's been underperforming for years. Leaders who are willing to directly address lingering issues, those concerns which are just below the surface, cultivate higher trust levels.

*Taking The Heat*
*"The people you challenge will test your steadiness and judge your worthiness by your response to their anger, not unlike teenagers, who want to know that they can blow hot without blowing their parents away. Receiving people's anger without becoming personally defensive generates trust. If you can hold steady*

*enough, remaining respectful of their pains and defending your perspective without feeling you must defend yourself, you may find that in the ensuing calm, relationships become stronger."*[3]

When we begin leading adaptive change, we wade into the deep waters of leadership. We become disturbers of the peace, upsetting the status quo. Every church has its own culture, along with familiar ways of doing what they do. When this is challenged, even for very good purposes, we can expect push-back. How leaders manage themselves then, when the heat turns up, will raise or lower trust. The congregation is watching to see if their leaders can take the heat without self-destructing or imploding.

*"Your management of an attack, more than the substance of the accusation, determines your fate."*[4]

When we manage the heat well, the push-back on adaptive changes, then disciples perceive us as trustworthy. We resist the temptation to attack or make the conversation personal. We receive the attack, without paying back kind for kind. We stay focused on the issues and initiatives, rather than lapsing into personality-critique or personal attack. Those observing come away from these interactions with greater respect for leaders. Increased trust is not far behind.

## **CULTIVATING VISION**

What's compelling about your future-vision for planet earth? In other words, does your faith tradition hold within it a compelling, hope-filled vision for what can happen in this world? As I'm writing this, another mass shooting occurred, this one politically motivated. Now, in 2017, these type events are commonplace. There was a time when we believed these kinds of events did not occur in the United States. Yet, our brokenness as human beings is ever more blatant. This leaves many of us asking what solutions are available.

As I'm writing this, there are great signs of hope alongside the brokenness of humankind. I'm sitting here in my t-shirt our family ordered soon after the shooting at Emmanuel AME Church in Charleston, SC. Extended family members of several who were slain put together an organization focused on one statement: "Hate Won't Win."[1] Never before has our family bought matching t-shirts, but this time we couldn't resist. We want to partner with others in our world who are determined to engage love as our primary weapon against hate.

So, as I embrace these two insights – the brokenness of humanity and the belief that love is stronger than hate – I find myself wondering how much I believe love can actually overcome hate. Do I find this belief in the Christian gospel? Is this the Way of Jesus – practicing love? Does this way of life have the power within it to change this world? How much am I willing to risk my comfort, lifestyle, family's security, and even myself on this belief?

Ultimately, how compelling is my version of the Christian story? Can it change this crazy world for the better?

Well, I guess these kinds of questions could launch us into some of the great theological debates of Christian history. Some Christ-followers believe that God's plan is to ultimately destroy this planet with fire, burning it to a cinder, yet rescuing the saved just before the big burn takes place. Others believe God's hopes and dreams include reclaiming this planet, renewing it into a "new Jerusalem" wherein its inhabitants experience harmony with God, each other, and the earth. How one understands eschatology influences one's view on the end game for planet earth. Either way, when it comes to visioning, we must consider what we believe God has in mind for our world.

The purpose of this book is not to engage end time debates, but instead to consider the nature of our visioning as churches. Over time, the Lord's Prayer as recorded in Matthew 6:9-13 has become my guide for visioning. Jesus clearly communicates that praying for the kingdom of God to come on earth as it is in heaven is how we should pray. This indicates that Jesus believes it's possible for God's kingdom to come more fully on earth than it currently is. Does this mean God's kingdom will ultimately come in full to planet earth? I believe so. I don't claim to know exactly how this will happen (whether burning is involved or not), but I'm firmly invested in the hope that God's will shall be done. This means that God's end game is to renew, transform, redeem, and recreate this planet. All the earth's inhabitants will someday join a common community, organized around the Lord of Lords and King of Kings. This end game for planet earth is a beautiful picture of harmony, peace, joy, and love in the full presence of God. What a vision for planet earth. There is no way I want to miss out on a movement which contributes to this kind of forward progress among human beings. I believe that's called the Christian Movement.

**What To Avoid**
Given this life-giving, hope-filled Movement of which we are part, what's going on with visioning in congregations? As we listen to

disciples in congregations, we frequently hear them make statements like, "O no, not another visioning project. We are still trying to recover from the last one. All our energy went into designing it, not to mention the high cost of the outside consultant. No way do we want to repeat that process." Typically these kinds of statements are accompanied by plenty of eye rolling and deep sighing. What's that about? I'm a very visionary person who grows excited when we engage in future-talk, dreaming about God's movement in our community and among us as congregations. Plenty of disciples in congregations are visionary people, along with their pastors. So what's the hesitation and reluctance about? With some reflection, we recognize the deficits in traditional visioning process models leave congregations flat and exhausted. Simultaneously, we need compelling visions to help us move ahead with clarity and direction. So let's pause, identifying particular traditional visioning related activities to avoid before we ever begin visioning in congregations. By first identifying them, clearing them away, our energy for visioning will rise dramatically.

*Let's avoid boring, wordy, churchy mission statements*
Up until around the turn of this century, too many churches still had mission statements which were significant theological treatises. They were lengthy paragraphs, if not pages, dragging on and on. The wording was church-based, requiring a fairly sophisticated level of theological understanding to make sense of this church's mission. Typically these mission statements were found attached to the constitution and by-laws or in a dusty folder on the bottom shelf of the deserted church library. No one used this kind of mission statement. No one cared about them. We created and preserved them, believing we must have a mission statement. Practically though, no one cared much about them. Can you imagine convincing your congregation to invest the time and energy required to repeat that experience?

*Let's avoid creating a vision which is largely self-focused*
Unfortunately, too many visioning processes have resulted in strategic ministry plans describing how we will be a wonderful church when we accomplish the vision. Examples of initiatives

when this is the case are:

- To fill our sanctuary with worshippers
- To reach and exceed our budget needs
- To build more buildings

There is a place for organizational development, upgrading and improving ourselves organizationally. Yet, when this is the primary focus of our vision, we indulge in the belief that it's all about us. Sure there is room in the vision for upgrading our facilities and developing our stewardship, yet these are ministry tools rather than ministry goals. The vision is how we and our communities will be different/better as a result of our partnership with God.

*Let's avoid visions we could accomplish while sleeping*
Uninspiring, unchallenging, unimaginative...these are vision descriptors to avoid. Since visioning can be messy or even contentious, some congregations default to the least common denominator. The result is a tepid and uninspiring vision. In an effort to resolve the tension between competing perspectives, compromises lead to a vision without much challenge. The result is low level inspiration, or even boredom and apathy. We could accomplish that vision while sleep-walking, like some churches do. Later we will explore what makes a vision motivating.

*Let's avoid a vision which codifies our outdated church paradigm*
During the Modern Era (up until about 2000AD), the typical outcome of congregational visioning processes was to take what we previously did as a church, import it into the present, followed by applying more vigor and energy to doing the same thing. In essence, we were codifying our church paradigm by capturing it in our strategic visioning plan, committing to practicing it more vigorously. Unfortunately, this approach discourages creativity and innovation, increasing the odds that adaptive failure will result.

As your congregation engages visioning, pay attention. When you sense you are drifting toward any of the practices identified above, stop and change direction. Farmers clearly identify the boundaries beyond which they don't want to plow when turning up the field. Similarly, these unhelpful visions to avoid can serve as markers for our visioning work. These visions to avoid help us stay in the flow of productive visioning.

**The Vision We Need**
*"Vision creation is almost always a messy, difficult, and sometimes emotionally charged exercise."*[2]

I'm remembering the look on his face. We were training clergy from various denominations toward leading their congregations effectively. This day we focused on visioning, presenting the following perspective with the following power point slide and subsequent quote.

Dangers of visioning
- Unbalances the system
- Changes the identity
- Leadership grows more vulnerable
- Loss of members or destructive acting-out

*"(Leaders) They must challenge those who lack the courage to move forward due to a lack of faith or an inability to share in the vision They must be able to 'speak truth to power' if necessary. And, at times, they must have the courage of conviction to choose the vision over relationships. Rarely will a congregation that embraces a new vision bring everyone along. Congregations that insist on 'not losing anyone' as they move forward in realizing the vision will only succeed in failing."*[3]

We discussed the reality of visioning. Latent congregational issues can often rise to the surface when we begin exploring our vision. Like the farmer who discovers toxicity in the soil only after scratching off the surface with the plow, congregational angst lurking below the surface is exposed when we open communication channels during visioning. The danger risk rises when we engage visioning. During the training mentioned before, we quickly moved to the following power point slide.

Dangers of not visioning
- Congregational lethargy & spiritual decline
- Loss of members or destructive acting- out
- Leadership grows more vulnerable
- Abdication of the leadership function
- Unfaithfulness to one's calling

The pastor mentioned before with the "aha" look on his face shared that during his long tenure in ministry, no one had ever shared about the dangers of visioning **and** not visioning. Perhaps we intuitively know this in congregations, yet we typically avoid the subject. There are risks when we engage visioning work, opening ourselves to challenging engagement. On the other hand, the dangers inherent in avoiding visioning are just as risky, perhaps more so. We are suggesting that visioning is one of the key cultivations when it comes to readying the congregation for adaptive change. Many of the other six key cultivations need the vision clearly articulated and embraced in order to gain traction.

So what we are looking for is not the tired, old visioning processes which lead to stale, flat, uninspiring visions. We've had enough of those in our collective journeys as congregations. In addition, we know that visioning heightens risk in congregations, though the risks inherent in visioning are preferable to those resulting from a lack of vision. So what are we looking for when it comes to visioning in congregations?

*We need aspirational visions*
*"To sustain momentum through a period of difficult change, you have to find ways to remind people of the orienting value – the positive vision – that makes the current angst worthwhile."*[4]

We all aspire to something. Christ-followers aspire to become the fullest expression of the person God wishes them to be. We believe God wants good for us, as well as having purposes for us to fulfill. We want to live into God's dream for our lives, becoming who God is calling us to become. We have aspirations as Christ followers.

During Making The Shift Weekends we invite participants into an aspirational activity. Shift presents three pathways for forward movement for individual disciples and congregations as a whole. Two of these pathways are developing disciples and becoming missional. We invite participants to imagine themselves and their congregations one year from now when they are further down each of these pathways. One year from now, when we are more fully disciples than we are now, what will we observe in our lives? What will we see ourselves doing? When we can honestly say we are greater disciples than we were a year ago, how will we know? How will our congregation be different and what will be doing when we are collectively greater disciples of Jesus? Part two of this activity is do the same kind of visioning regarding becoming missional individuals and missional churches. How will I know I am more missional one year from now? How will we know as a congregation that we are more missional one year from now? What will we observe ourselves doing which indicates we are more missional than we were one year ago? Here are examples of answers participants have given when we invite them to share with the large group.

*"People are drawn to Christ, submitting their lives to Jesus Christ, discovering hope"*
*"People with very secular belief systems are drawn to the exceptional hospitality, love, and community found in this church"*
*"Powerful experiences of God's presence in worship"*
*"Signs of the kingdom; things happen which are beyond human explanation"*
*"Groups of disciples are called to launch out, infiltrating their context and subcultures, establishing missional faith communities"*
*"We as a church will actively forgive and pursue reconciliation with others, bringing a new spirit of forgiveness to our faith community"*
*"Our focus as a congregation will be the New Commandment, organizing our lives around love"*
*"We will work to advance God's healing of our society and planet"*
*"We will contribute to the spiritual journey of others whom we encounter each day"*
*"We will practice hospitality, especially with those who are left out, dispossessed or unlike us"*

These visions are aspirational. We are not there yet, but we can visualize becoming these individual disciples and collective congregations. We need aspirational visions which describe how we will rise up and participate in God's reclamation project in our world. When we identify Spirit-inspired aspirations, we find ourselves leaning forward, pushing ourselves to grow and develop into more robust Christ-following congregations. We are called to move into the gap between where we currently are and to where God is calling us.

*We need compelling visions*
Why are you part of this Christian Movement? How much do you believe the gospel of Jesus Christ has the power within it to transform this world toward the good? How much does this world need the good news of Christ? Essentially, how compelling is your vision of God's kingdom coming on earth as it is in heaven?

When our vision is more people believing in Jesus and then escaping this world with good fire insurance, then we are truncating the gospel. When our vision is Christ-followers secluding themselves, avoiding interaction with the world around them as much as possible, we are living in fear. When our vision is spending nearly all our collective money to keep our institution running, then few people will be gravitate toward our expression of Christianity.

On the other hand, when we believe the gospel of Jesus Christ is the best hope for this world, then we are discovering a compelling vision. When we imagine the kingdom of God infiltrating the fallen systems and structures of our world, transforming them toward justice, then we want to participate. When our attitudes, actions, and relationships are transformed by the gospel this side of heaven, then we are hungry for Jesus Christ. When we see lives of neighbors and community partners being enriched because of our participation, then we want to do even more. When eternal life through Christ is a quality of life now as well as quantity of life in the future, then we are encouraged. The gospel of Jesus Christ is compelling when we identify its nature and application to our world.

Given the condition of our world, along with our culture's low toleration for meaningless activities, anything less than a compelling vision will not sustain motivated engagement. When we discern our compelling vision, it serves to further adaptive change in three ways.

First, we are drawn into a movement. Compelling visions motivate us to act, captivating our collective imaginations. Every time I watch a video of Martin Luther King Jr's *I Have A Dream* speech, I'm caught up in his compelling vision of greater racial harmony in the USA. The speech inspires the best in who we are to rise to the surface, invigorating us toward joining the racial reconciliation movement. Second, due to the losses, tension, and uncomfortableness which change brings, the vision has to be worth its inherent challenges. We are asking disciples in congregations to give up familiar and cherished ways of being church. In order to do so, they must be convinced that we are called into a better way of being church. Compelling visions give us the courage to overcome the inherent barriers to vision-actualization. We are willing to sacrifice the current comfortable status quo in exchange for a future preferable church. Third, compelling visions strengthen our perseverance, equipping us to delay gratification. We humans are able to set aside our personal preferences and comforts when we believe in the vision we are pursuing. We can delay enjoying the fruits of our labor for a worthy cause. Compelling visions function in at least these three ways, giving us the motivation to get up and out the door, partnering with God toward the kingdom's actualization this side of heaven.

*We need missionally-focused visions*
"What is God's calling for us in this next season of ministry and mission?"
This question is where traditional visioning and strategic planning processes focus. We want to identify our major initiatives to pursue over the next 2-4 years through answering this question. Some very useful outcomes can result from this beginning point, yet some obvious limitations are inherent as well.

Without great plowing of the spiritual and paradigmatic ground before hand, this question often leads to churches remaining within their current church model, with slight tune-ups in terms of quality and commitment. Attractional churches (most all are) find this approach very familiar and comfortable.

The missional church movement is pushing our perspectives away from ourselves toward God and this world. God's desire, it appears from scripture, is to bring the kingdom to earth as it is in heaven (see Lord's Prayer). It appears as if God actually intends to actualize the kingdom of God here, this side of heaven, before it's all done. We are recognizing that God's mission is larger and more expansive than our church. God's focus is more on saving the entire world than saving any one particular local church. We will discover our "salvation" through shifting our focus from ourselves to God's mission; reconciling, healing, and transforming the world around us. That's where the action is; the center of God's activity in this world...."thy kingdom come, thy will be done on earth as it is in heaven." Asking us to pray this way was not busy-work to keep us occupied until Jesus' return. No, inherent in this prayer is the call to action; joining God's efforts to transform this world toward the kingdom.

So, let's start there. Let's begin our visioning with questions centered in God's mission; God's hopes and dreams for humankind and our planet rather than focusing on ourselves. Outcomes of this kind of visioning may be:
*"Malnutrition and hunger in the children attending the elementary school next door to our church campus will be eradicated."*
*"A new missionally –focused worshipping community will rise up and take shape in the subdivision near our church campus."*
*"Every disciple in our congregation will be able to articulate his/her sense of call for this season of life."*
*"Forty more adults in our community will be reading well enough to pass the GED exam."*
*"A cadre of men from this congregation will be engaging other men in the recovery program with whom we partner."*
*"Our community partnership fund will distribute three times its current annual amount to our community partners."*
*"Every disciple in our congregation will be engaged with a disciple-*

*developing small group, facilitating spiritual growth."*
This is missionally-focused visioning, leading to an exciting pathway forward for our congregations. Later in this chapter we will describe questions to guide our discernment as we become more missional.

*We need organic visions*
When farmers "go organic," they often discover many resources inherent in their growing environment which they previously overlooked. Given the availability of pesticides and other growing aids at the market, some farmers simply don't see the resources already present in their context. Manure from various animals helps particular crops grow. Compost with particular mixtures nourishes the growth of other particular plants. Within the growing environment one finds much of what's needed for a healthy and bountiful harvest.

There was a time in the life of the Church (Modern Era) when experts from outside our churches could arrive with the answers. They would describe particular programs or best practices from elsewhere. Since culture was more homogenous then, transporting ministry approaches from elsewhere and dropping them into another church context worked….enough. Now that culture is deforming right before our eyes, we recognize approaches which are effective elsewhere are just that…effective elsewhere. We can still learn from the way other churches approach their calling, yet each church is unique, existing in its own cultural context. Thus, we don't need another expert to drop the next best program on our church. God's hopes and dreams for us are going to be discerned by the people closest to the action – those who are each particular church. It's time to trust God's movement among us, allowing the fruits of the Spirit rise up among us from within.

When we discover our vision, it serves to focus and guide our efforts. There are so many worthy moves any congregation could make. The vision narrows our focus, guiding our efforts toward making our best contribution to God's reclamation project on planet earth. Now we turn to the key practices for cultivating vision.

## Key Practices For Cultivating Vision

Cultivating vision is a key practice which plays out differently than the other six. Not only do we want to cultivate vision, but also engage in visioning. Cultivation is the first step, yet we recommend moving on to completing the visioning work as part of this cultivation process. We need the vision clearly articulated because a compelling, aspirational vision is one of the drivers motivating adaptive change. Many other key practices are driven by the vision, requiring clarity about where we are going. So the following key practices include cultivation work, but also vision identification.

*Start with God*
This sounds silly. As already noted, we typically begin visioning by asking what God's calling is for us. Though this is a helpful question in its fitting place, it's not the place to begin. When we start here, we are focusing more on ourselves than on God. Instead we want to begin by increasing our understanding of God's intentions for this world. So we cultivate vision in the congregation by first focusing in on the greatest expression of God this world has seen: Jesus Christ. Engage congregational leadership in study, reflection, and dialogue regarding the ministry of Jesus in the gospels. Since the kingdom of God was the prominent theme in Jesus teaching, study the nature of this kingdom. What does it look like, as described by Jesus? What's its nature? What are the Biblical examples of the kingdom? Rather than assume we know these answers, start fresh, engaging leaders in focused learning regarding Jesus and his mission.

Since this Christian movement is over 2000 years old by now, there is layer upon layer of interpretation of Jesus' movements and teachings as we find them in the gospels. Most of us come to the gospels with plenty of baggage along with all kinds of assumptions about what Jesus really was about. For this reason, we need a fresh view, immersing ourselves in the words and ways of Jesus. Ask your questions, explore the meaning, challenge your assumptions, and even consult the experts as needed. We want as clear an understanding of Jesus and the way of life to which he calls us as possible.

*Distill the call of God into a high level mission statement*
When we thoroughly engage in exploration of Jesus and his mission, it is a very short step to a high level mission statement. The amount of time it takes to identify this statement should be one-tenth of the time we invested in learning about Jesus and the kingdom. By high level we mean brief and broad. This mission statement is not a strategic plan, nor a doctrinal statement, nor major initiatives. Rather this mission statement captures the essence of God's mission with which we are partnering. Here are examples.

- Making Christ known in God's community
- Making disciples for the transformation of the world
- Loving God, loving others, loving ourselves
- Joining God's transformation project

*Engage in focused exploration of what it may look like for the kingdom coming more fully in our community and church*
How will we know when God's kingdom comes more fully in our community and/or in our congregation? What will we see taking place? What would be the specific changes we would see when Jesus' way of life takes hold more fully? When we are living more fully into our mission statement which is based on our understanding of the kingdom, how will our community be different? Cultivating this step requires community engagement. Knowing our community well enough that we can identify where the Spirit is already moving, along with where the places of brokenness reside, is necessary.

Pay attention to how your leaders answer the questions above. There are nearly an infinite number of opportunities for partnering with God in our communities and in our congregations. So when congregational leaders start describing opportunities, they are sharing their discernment. What they describe is where their passion and engagement is connecting. Major initiatives can flow directly from these descriptions of God's anticipated movement in your community and congregation. Narrow these initiatives down to a number which you can engage at this time in your congregation's progress; perhaps four to six.

*Collectively commit to this vision*
Is there ever perfect discernment and articulation of a congregation's vision? Not likely; but not to worry. As we move ahead in mission and ministry, God is certainly able to redirect us as needed. So now comes the time when we are poised to affirm and celebrate the vision. There are several important ways to do this. First, use your congregation's decision-making process as described in your polity. Make sure the vision moves through the proper channels so that there is no question about it becoming the accepted and confirmed vision to pursue. Second, publicize the vision thoroughly in the congregation, making sure everyone who is so inclined understands the nature of this vision. Third, celebrate vision discernment in the context of worship, including commitment. Publicly committing ourselves is one way to strengthen our resolve when implementing and living the vision grows challenging.

*Cascade the vision through the entire congregation*
I realize that using this language ("cascade") suggests that vision identification is done by leaders followed by sharing with the congregation. In our vision identification work over the years, we typically have worked hard to gather the input of each disciple in the congregation. We still believe in this approach, yet recognize that a leadership team is needed to approve the vision. Congregations with congregational polity will also work through a team of people who shepherd the vision process. Regardless of one's polity, after confirming the vision comes the time for identifying every individual and group's part in implementing the vision. Living the vision is a group endeavor with each individual disciple along with every team in the congregation doing their part. Though our particular actions will shift and change over time, we want to identify our current actions which will contribute to vision actualization. This positions us well for supporting each other as we move forward. We can invite each other to enter into healthy accountability relationships around the vision's actualization as well.

*Make vision actualization your highest priority*
The previous practices for cultivating vision are arranged sequentially. Now, congregational leaders are positioned for

leading vision implementation. This vision is what we use to guide most everything we do from this point onward. When it comes to setting the agenda for staff and lay leadership team meetings, the vision informs the agenda. When it comes to determining priorities between lay leadership team meetings, the vision guides us. Each meeting we can share our progress, identify the obstacles which held us back, and plan the next steps for implementing the vision. When the finance team prepares the budget, the vision becomes a major guide for allocating funds. Even more, the vision equips us to say yes or no to opportunities as they arise.

*Look for the compelling, aspirational, missionally-focused, organic vision*

Periodically in the process described above, put your foot on the brake and step back. Pause to consider how much the emerging vision reflects what we need from a vision. Using the descriptive words above, assess the vision's development. This is a way to check ourselves as we vision. When the vision satisfies each of the descriptors above, then we are more likely to discover a vision which serves its purpose.

# CULTIVATING LEADERSHIP

Remember John Wayne? As a child, I enjoyed sitting with my dad, watching those old Western movies. John Wayne was the epitome of the heroic lone western warrior who would swoop in and save the day. The central characteristics of the lone hero archetype (nearly always male) were perfectly combined in his larger than life on-screen persona. Through John Wayne and other on-screen personalities, a generation of leaders in the USA was taught to believe this is what leadership looks like.

Though we have grown beyond that outdated perspective, plenty of clergy still view pastoral leadership as a solo activity. Remnants of the lone warrior with all the answers and strength beyond measure linger. Except in the most dictatorial church contexts, most of us clergy learn quickly that leadership in the church is a shared endeavor. In fact, leading churches requires far more sophisticated leadership skills and competencies than plenty of other leadership opportunities. But this chapter is not only about pastoral leadership. Instead we are suggesting that adaptive change in congregations requires a leadership team, a cadre of leaders committed to cultivating deep change. The lone hero, strong man approach to leadership in congregations has largely gone the way of all things. Instead we are looking for leaders who can cultivate the leadership capacity of congregations, increasing the likelihood of adaptive change.

**Leading Congregations**
Before focusing on cultivating leadership who can lead adaptive

change, we will do well to recognize the nature of leading in church. Certainly leadership is leadership, wherever it's present. On the other hand, leading congregations is a unique endeavor. Participants in churches are not there to earn a paycheck, to move up in their career, or to gain status. The levers leaders in other organizations employ are not available to church leaders. Connecting with the motivation of participants sufficiently when it comes to leading change requires great insight, spiritual depth, and effective leadership skills. We need the same leadership skills and competencies of leaders in other organizations, plus more. So before we grow specific about cultivating leaders toward adaptive change, let's consider the nature of church leadership. The following insights will help orient us to the challenge ahead.

*Leadership will happen in your congregation*
Every system, whether governmental, educational, corporate, familial, or communal will generate sufficient leadership for itself. If not, that system will cease to exist, or at least deconstruct to a previously unrecognizable form. This means that every congregational system needs sufficient leadership to function. To function well or effectively, every congregation needs more than sufficient leadership. This also means that pastoral and lay leaders are called on to function as leaders. The congregational system needs leadership, with that leadership ideally flowing from those in recognized positions of leadership.

Astute congregational leaders will also read between these lines to recognize that leadership will rise up from somewhere in the congregation when identified leaders do not lead. Now, I'm not describing dictatorial or autocratic leadership. I am suggesting that leadership is a functional requirement for systems to operate. The system will find the leadership it needs from somewhere in order to function. Healthy leadership in congregations occurs when the identified leaders function as leaders. So when we find ourselves in leadership positions in congregations, we are there with purpose. The church needs us to step up and function well. When we do not, for whatever reason, leadership will rise up from somewhere else in the system. Typically when this happens, things do not go well. Creating leadership vacuums through non-functional leadership invites power grabs, acting-out, and passive-aggressive behavior. One of the greatest tools for conflict prevention is making the decision to lead, followed by actually leading well. When formal leaders don't lead, expect leadership to happen anyway, usually in unhelpful ways.

*Leadership in congregations is predictably transitional*
When coaching clergy and consulting churches, we regularly hear them express concern about their fruit basket leadership turnover each year. One third of the formal leaders rotate off the lay leadership team each year, making room for new leaders and avoiding consolidation of power. So while this approach is helpful, it is also unhelpful. High investment in training and acculturation is required to get these new leaders up to speed.

Pastors and church staff are also transitional. Though this is more true in some denominations than others, yet pastors and staff come and go in all congregations. Given this, we may as well accept the fact that leadership in congregations is transitional; always. This means that we must work toward clarity in role and function of our leaders. Leaders need to know their role and be able to articulate how they function in this particular congregation in order to maintain congregational momentum. Later we will discuss a Leadership Team Covenant; a very helpful tool to create cohesive culture among leaders. This helps avoid the losses, while continuing forward movement, when leadership transitions.

*Congregational leaders cannot not lead*
It's funny. Periodically I will hear a lay leader describing his/her interaction with a disciple in the congregation, claiming they were speaking as just another disciple rather than from their leadership role. I'm sorry, but leadership doesn't work that way. When we become leaders in the congregation, we are always leaders, even when we prefer not to be. Sometimes pastors long for the opportunity to engage people in their communities without them knowing they are pastors. These pastors recognize that as soon as someone knows their vocational role, immediately this vocational role becomes a major dynamic in the relationship. This is also true for lay leaders. In meetings, gatherings, and

conversations, leaders are always representing the congregation, like it or not. Given this, we may as well accept our role as leaders, knowing it's with us in all congregational interactions. Congregational leaders cannot not lead as they engage their congregations.

*Leadership in congregations is developmental*
There's a huge canyon between implementing ministry and stewarding the vision. Larry Osborne, in *Sticky Teams,* describes the development of their lay leadership team as their church numerically grew.[1] Stage One was Doing. This is the "all hands on deck" stage of church leadership wherein the lay leadership team functions more like a committee. Each team member is tasked with implementing ministry through a certain part of the church (Spiritual Nurture, Disciple Care, etc.). Stage Two is Approving. Small to mid-size churches may grow to where more leadership is needed. The leadership team shifts its role toward approving activities and making decisions. No longer is their primary function implementing the ministry of the church, but to guide and approve. Stage Three is Reviewing. The workload grows too great in Stage Two, with the lay leadership team bogging down, becoming a bottle neck for progress. In Stage Three the lay leaders review what is happening and recommend changes as needed. They are still involved in major decisions, yet their role is to steward the aspirational vision of the congregation, maintaining congruence in direction and focus. When we look through the developmental lens at congregational leadership, then we are empowered to consider shifting our roles as needed by our particular congregation.

*Leadership is always shaping culture*
Whatever gets the most airtime, the most communication, is what we grow to believe is significant. As leaders lead, they are always shaping the culture and values of their congregation. When leaders regularly focus on items like budget, worship attendance, and building maintenance, then the congregation is led to believe these institutional concerns are what's really important when it comes to being church. When the leaders focus on transformed lives, spiritual growth, and community transformation, then the congregation grows to believe this is what's important in our

communal lives. Wherever we focus our attention, whatever we lift up regularly, whatever drives our lay leadership team agendas...these become our priorities over time.

So, leaders beware. Take a very close look at what occupies your time and energy. Examine the stories you tell, the activities you highlight, and the content of your reports. Whatever these are is what your church will grow to value over time. Congregations are always learning about what is important here in church. Leaders are always shaping their answer through their focus. Choose carefully, knowing we are constantly shaping our congregation's culture, values, and trajectory.

**Faith Change Agent**
The insights just noted describe the leadership milieu in congregations overall. There are particular seasons in the life of the Church when a particular kind of leadership is needed. As already noted, we are in a season of high change, moving from the Modern to Postmodern Era. God's Church needs different kinds of leaders than it did before, when conditions in the growing environment were different. Now that everything is changing, what pastoral and lay leadership images are fitting guides?

To answer this question, we begin with our context. First we ask just what our world needs from God's Church in this 21$^{st}$ century. Well, on one hand, the world needs exactly what it's always needed...the gospel of Jesus Christ. This primal call of the Church has not changed. On the other hand, the world needs the Church to relate to it in ways with which it can resonate. This means relevance. Our congregations must discover how to engage their local communities in ways which open doors to encounters with God. Previously (Modern Era) we were ministering in a period of continuous, yet slower change. Culture in the USA was homogeneous enough to discover "standardized" ways of being church which were transportable from community to community. Now (Postmodern Era) we live in a period of discontinuous, radical reformation for the Church and most other of society's institutions and organizations. Structural upheaval and systemic shifts are common rather than exceptional. Looking around at the type of world leaders finding their way into governmental positions is a clear indication that culture as we have known it is shifting. This is the world the Church inhabits as well, requiring churches to re-form their paradigms for being church. If we believe the gospel is good news, why would we not adapt the way we express the gospel to what opens doors for spiritual pilgrims in our communities?

Second, we ask what the Church needs from its leadership in order to adapt to its context. Those who have been part of congregations during the Modern Era recognize certain images guiding pastoral leadership like the Statesman, Chaplain, and Entrepreneur. Each of these approaches to pastoring was effective and helpful during the Modern Era. Yet, now that we are in the "Great Migration," as Brian McLaren calls it, we need a different kind of leadership in congregations.[2]

Congregations are caught up in the same developmental challenge as other societal institutions and organizations; adapting to the world in which we live. We are transitioning into new expressions of church even as we speak. Some churches won't make it, finding the transitions required beyond their capacity. Others will develop the kind of leadership needed to adapt to the new weather patterns in their growing environment.

A new pastoral and lay leader guiding image is rising up to help us describe what we need from congregational leaders to effectively make this shift to the Postmodern world in which we live: **Faith Change Agent.** We are suggesting that congregations need pastoral and lay leaders to adopt who understand their primary calling as helping us move from here to there; to transition well, adapting as we go. This is what congregations need now. By embracing the Faith Change Agent pastoral and lay leadership image, congregational leaders will more likely apply their leadership to what's needed. Let's explore this image further.

First, everything we do as disciples and congregations is centered in our faith. Our understanding of God and God's ways, our trust in God, our worldview…each of these are components of our faith. Congregational leaders who live into this new image start from faith. Faith is the foundation, motivation, and guidance system for their leadership. They speak the language of faith when framing the leadership challenges before us. They work to draw our faith to the surface when we are facing problems. They challenge us to put our faith into action, generating innovative practices. They encourage us to trust the Holy Spirit, who leads us into creative adaptation. Though they may use leadership principles and practices from the world around us, they translate them into our indigenous language and native culture: faith.

Second, these pastoral and lay leaders view their primary calling as change. Effective, mission-congruent change is the greatest need of established congregations; and subsequently exactly what we need from our leaders. Certainly Faith Change Agents may use comfort, reminding us of our security in Christ, encourage stability where it's found and needed. Even so, their ultimate goal is to help us move from church-as-we-have-known-it to church-as-it-is-becoming. They see the focus of their calling as transitional; to help us transition into the church we need to become. Adaptive, healthy change is their aim. FCAs combine the faith journey with the change process, constructively leading our adaptation.

Third, these leaders integrate this Faith Change calling into their personal leadership self-image. All leaders function from internalized leadership images. Some see themselves as warriors while others see themselves as CEOs. Common pastoral leadership images were described above. Faith Change Agents believe they are called to this people for this time in the life of this congregation. They believe they are agents called to lead the adaptive change process. This is not only professional work for pastors or volunteer work for lay leaders. Perceiving one's role as FCA is personal, involving a sense of call. Faith Change Agents believe God has prepared them particularly for leading this congregation forward into adaptive change. Perhaps they pull from other leadership images like social movement organizer, group therapist, aspirational vision manager, positively-oriented parent, leadership coach, or holy provocateur. Yet, they see their core calling as congregational leaders in this 21$^{st}$ century as Faith Change Agents. These leaders are energized by the adaptive challenges ahead, yearning for the actualization of our aspirational, compelling vision.

**The Unique Role Of Pastors**
Though we believe congregations need Faith Change Agents leading them at this point in our developmental history, we don't recommend pastors and lay leaders claim this leadership image lightly. Leading adaptive change is not light duty. Before jumping into those waters, testing of the waters is helpful, using the following recommendations. Though these apply to lay leaders, we are focusing specifically now on the role of pastors in these recommendations.

*Check your calling, including your willingness and capacity to see the adaptive process through*
Wait a minute, this book is about cultivating readiness, not actually launching and implementing adaptive change. Though true, can you imagine readying a congregation through these seven key cultivations, followed by handing off to other leaders to make the adaptive moves? No, if we are going to be Faith Change Agents, readying the congregational system for adaptive moves, then the responsible approach to leadership is to remain in place to see the congregation through several major adaptive moves. Pastors or lay leaders who leave their congregations during these pivotal moments will remove necessary ingredients from the soil mix, lowering the quality of the crop.

Pastors considering cultivating adaptive change as Faith Change Agents must consider their sense of calling. "Am I called to these people who are this church? Am I committed to this congregation's present and future? Do I love them enough to embrace the call to cultivate readiness for adaptive change? Do I have the capacity to cultivate adaptive change, persevering when this work grows challenging?" The old wisdom, "Do not start what you cannot finish," applies. Readying the congregation for adaptive change is significant work, requiring much from the congregation itself. Responsible pastoral leaders don't initiate this kind of movement without the willingness to participate, seeing it through.

*Consider the readiness of your significant relationships for this kind of ministry*
How is the health of each of your significant relationships? Rarely are our relationships all we want them to be, yet before engaging this deep work in congregations we need enough stability in our relationships to allow energy and capacity for intense vocational involvement. We are not suggesting we can ignore our significant relationships. We are suggesting that when we are in a time of relational crisis is not the ideal time to begin cultivating adaptive change. Let's tend to our priorities first (personal significant relationships), then move to engaging the call to serve as Faith Change Agents.

*Invest in renewable energy sources*
What about you personally? How is your health…spiritual, physical, relational? Cultivating the growing environment which leads to adaptive change is not short-term nor light work. We will need endurance, stamina, patience, and commitment to lead effectively. We are not describing a sprint, but an endurance trail run. We will need water, energy bars, and rest breaks along the way. Life-giving spiritual disciplines and practices are sources of renewable energy. Regularly inquiring how it is with our souls renews us. Engaging with people who are soul gainers rather than drainers helps sustain us in our journeys. To provide sustained effective leadership for adaptive change we must have renewable energy sources in place.

Before we move on to cultivating leaders, there is one more very significant consideration when it comes to being Faith Change Agents. Every pastoral and lay leader has a disposition toward change. Attitudes, personality, biases, life experiences, and theology combine to form a disposition…a stance, if you will, toward change. In fact, these dispositions are not limited to individuals, but are present in the life of every organization, including congregations. Just below the surface our disposition toward change guides our interactions with change. With this in mind, consider the following chart contrasting two change dispositions.

| **Change Disposition** | |
|---|---|
| **Success oriented** | Failure avoidant |
| **Continuous risk-taking** | Avoiding costly mistakes |
| **Playing to win** | Playing not to lose |
| **Intensification of effort** | Conservation of effort |
| **Approaching the challenge** | Avoiding the challenge |
| **Promotion-focused** | Prevention-focused |
| **Taking initiative** | Pulling back |
| **Gain oriented** | Loss prevention oriented |
| **Learns from mistakes and moves on** | Dwells on mistakes as if terminal |
| **Driven by desire to achieve** | Driven by desire to avoid failure |

No change disposition description is completely descriptive of a particular leader, yet we will tend toward one side of this chart or the other. Obviously, anyone who takes up the Faith Change Agent image as guidance for their leadership will come face to face with this graphic. We invite you to pause, clear your thinking and feelings, and then look at this graphic again. Let's view it as a continuum, recognizing we may be anywhere from extreme left to right. As honestly as possible, place a dot on each item, identifying where you are in your relationship with change, followed by prayerful reflection.

**Key Practices For Cultivating Leaders**
Already this chapter has presented two excellent ways to cultivate the leadership we need in congregations to lead adaptive change. First we explored active dynamics in the congregational leadership milieu. Engaging this material with leaders raises their awareness about congregational leadership, while also clearly communicating, "You are in leadership now." Second, we described and recommended Faith Change Agent as the emerging

leadership image needed in this Postmodern Era Church. Engaging leaders around the FCA leadership image will directly lead them into adaptive change considerations. Congregations might consider a retreat or briefer learning experience engage FCA is a guiding image for their leadership. Many questions will be generated by presenting this image. "Why would we need to be FCAs? Why does the church need that much change? Do we have the spiritual energy for this kind of leadership?" Many questions will rise in this discussion. We want leaders to ask these questions, knowing this contributes to their development toward becoming leaders for adaptive change. Introducing the FCA image personalizes the challenges of leading adaptive change, drawing congregational leaders into robust consideration of their roles. This is one of the beginning places when introducing our leaders to adaptive change in congregations. Embracing this FCA image as our guiding image for our leadership positions us well for cultivating adaptive change in the growing environment. Now let's explore additional key practices toward cultivating leaders in the growing environment.

*Identify where leadership happens in your congregational system*
This statement sounds strange to the ears of some congregations. The polity of many churches requires a lay leadership team who partners with the pastor and church staff to lead the congregation. Most of these do a congregational meeting once each year in order to make decisions about very high level items, while also calling special congregational meetings when/if needed. Their polity explicitly identifies where leadership happens. Other congregations are more democratically organized, preferring congregational polity. Since these are my roots, I'm familiar with the strengths and weaknesses of congregational polity. Wonderfully, everyone in the congregation is invited to be part of the discernment process when setting direction and making decisions. This is an inclusive approach, taking the community of faith aspect of our faith very seriously. One challenge inherent therein is the dispersion of leadership. When the congregation is the ultimate authority under God, then who's in leadership? This congregational approach to being church provides a ripe context for authoritarian and dictatorial pastors and staff to grasp power. Strong personalities among lay persons

can collect great influence here. At the same time, other go to the other extreme, discovering no one is in charge. Leadership may be so dispersed that small groups (staffs, committees, teams) have to make their own way forward, leading to silo type ministry. These congregations don't have sufficient structures for focused leadership. Interestingly, many congregationally-based churches are now developing Leadership Councils or Elder Boards to help them with their leadership needs.

Another consideration when identifying where leadership happens in our congregations is the formal/informal leadership phenomenon. Often when consulting with congregations, we are informed who in the church must be on board with an initiative for it to pass. "When Mary speaks, everyone listens. So if she's on board with this, then it will go. If not, we may as well forget it." There are people of influence in every congregation. Most of the time, these people are influential because of the high trust they have earned through their consistent caring character over time. Occasionally they are congregational bullies whose influence is destructive. This is an entire other subject for another book! In the meantime, we want to recognize those informal leaders who are great gifts to our congregations, including them in cultivating the growing environment.

So, what are we to do when we find ourselves in congregations wherein we cannot clearly identify where focused leadership happens? Given our fast-paced ministry environments, we won't function well nor adapt effectively without recognized and endorsed leadership teams. If we cannot answer the question above, it's time to start this conversation, eventually resulting in an identified and formalized leadership team. Even if our answer turns out to be an amalgamation of several teams who form the leadership cadre, growing expressly clear about this is necessary for cultivating the growth environment.

*Strongly invite congregational leaders into leadership*
What do we say to those disciples who are called to be congregational leaders when they are ordained? What do we say when they are installed into their positions? In my experience, what holds many congregational leaders back is their lack of

awareness about their roles as leaders. Many do not seem to live with awareness that they are leaders in this congregation; or at least they are reluctant to embrace their leadership roles. I'm remembering one ordination sermon which included the strong statement, "Now, YOU ARE spiritual leaders for this church." We can't overstate the importance of accepting and embracing our roles as leaders. This holds true for pastors, church staff, and lay leaders.

The significance and influence of strong lay leadership played out before my eyes while listening to a report presented to a church from a consultant using the U.S. Congregational Life Survey. The consultant reported that first time visitors to congregations find their way to a particular church due to two influences above all others. First, they visit worship for the first time because of the location of the church campus. Proximity or familiarity make location important to people who visit worship for the first time. Second, they visit worship for the first time in response to an invitation from someone they know. The consultant went on to say that a person is six times more likely to visit a church due to an invitation from a disciple there rather than an invitation from the pastor. What's this about? Why such a high return on the disciple's invitation and low return on the pastor's? People expect the pastor to invite them, believing this is part of his/her job. They would be surprised if the pastor did not invite them to the pastor's church. Conversely, disciples from particular congregations are not required in any way to invite others. They do this of their own volition. This invitation carries more weight, since it's from a peer. Positive peer influence is powerful. Let's help leaders in our congregations accept and embrace their roles as leaders.

*Cultivate a faith-based understanding of leadership in congregational leaders*
We live in fascinating times when it comes to leadership. The need for Faith Change Agents is clear in this swiftly shifting environment where traditional models of leadership are growing less effective. Currently we are seeing extremely non-traditional types of leaders rise up in most every profession and institution. Some of these leaders are so extreme, they are obviously over-

reactions to what was lacking in the traditional leaders who went before. Often the tenure of these extremist leaders is short. At the same time, familiar models of leadership are deforming while new expressions of leadership are rising.

During this leadership model transition, congregational leaders need a clearer understanding of Jesus-shaped leadership than before. We can easily grow confused; coming to believe the kinds of leadership we see in our culture are the kinds of leaders needed in congregations. Nothing is farther from the truth. In fact, even the original disciples struggled with their role as leaders in this Jesus-focused movement. Three of the four gospels describe a request from James and his brother John regarding their place in the pecking order of Jesus' leadership cadre. They asked to be the left and right hand leaders when Jesus comes into his messiahship, much like cabinet members flanking a United States president. Their understanding of leadership includes great glory, fame, and honor. When the other disciples hear their very bold request, they grow furious. Glory-seeking behavior leads to jealousy and division in groups. Jesus observes what's happening and quickly intervenes, calling the disciples together, instructing them.

> *"You know that among the Gentiles those whom they recognize as their rulers lord it over them, and their great ones are tyrants over them. But it is not so among you; but whoever wishes to become great among you must be your servant, and whoever wishes to be first among you must be slave of all. For the Son of Man came not to be served but to serve,"*
>
> Mark 10:42-45a

There it is; that servant image Jesus frequently describes and demonstrates for the disciples. Those who are people of influence in the community gathered around Jesus are those with servant attitudes and actions. Their goal is to contribute to the lives of others, helping them along life's pathway. Christian leaders are not in it for glory or attention, but for the benefit of those they serve. One way leaders serve is helping the congregation live into its calling as fully as possible. The focus is on the growth, development, and progress of those we serve, rather than on the status of those who lead. Leading in this context actually is giving away attention, encouragement, and affirmation; building up others. This is the shape of congregational leadership as described by Jesus. So don't assume congregational leaders see their roles through the servant lens. Instead assume they are at least partially culturally influenced by the leadership models prevalent in our society. Cultivating adaptive change includes cultivating leaders toward servanthood, shepherding the congregation toward joining God's mission more fully.

*Do the Readiness Indicator with congregational leaders, followed by learning adaptive change concepts*
After identifying where leadership happens and who the leaders currently are, we turn to the scriptures, gaining a clear understanding of the nature of leadership in this faith community context. Then we are positioned for looking at our particular expression of church. Before even beginning to describe the need for adaptive change, we suggest congregational leaders complete the Readiness Indicator in *Farming Church*. Through completing this Indicator before engaging the *Farming Church* content, we can assess where our congregation currently is in its readiness for adaptive change. Many leaders will complete the Indicator before reading the book, given its position near the books' beginning. If they have not completed the Indicator, encourage leaders to complete it at any point in the cultivation process. The Readiness Indicator itself is a strong tool for raising the readiness quotient in itself.

Now, leaders in a congregation are positioned for discussing the four key practices of Adaptive Change Theory in *Farming Church*. Pastors, church staffs, and lay leadership teams can easily make discussion of Adaptive Change concepts part of their regularly scheduled meetings. On the other hand, those who do a Farming Church Retreat will learn these concepts together in a more focused way.

*Develop and implement your support plan with congregational leaders*
Just as farming is a year round occupation, requiring sustained

effort and perseverance over time, so is cultivating and leading adaptive change. We are inviting congregational leaders into more than business as usual. Now is the time in the Church when we are travelling from familiar Egypt through the unfamiliar wilderness. We are forgetting what lies behind and focusing on the upward call of God in Christ Jesus. We need effective Faith Change Agents who can help shepherd us into emerging expressions of God's Church. This kind of congregational leadership is atypical and abnormal...in a very good and healthy sense. Given the intensity of this work, we will need sufficient and robust support to maintain our leadership focus and effort. Readying leaders to lead adaptive change includes consistently supporting them as they lead.

Since adapting well can be a matter of life or death for our congregations, developing and implementing our support plan for those in the thick of change is necessary. Please consider the following recommendations for your support plan. These are not prescriptive, yet are significant areas of focus we believe are necessary to address.

- Describe the pastors' relationships with congregational leaders. A primary leadership activity for the pastor is to support other congregational leaders as they lead adaptive change efforts. This means pastors personally developing supportive one-to-one relationships with congregational leaders, regularly investing in their overall well-being.
- Every congregational leader has a coach or mentor. Some congregations use our Disciple Developing Coaching approach for supporting each other.[3] Whatever your approach, we recommend each congregational leader has a coach or mentor to walk with them as they lead.
- Regularly involve congregational leaders in learning opportunities. Leaders who consistently invest in learning tend to be more energized, enthusiastic, and engaged. Learning opportunities, like annual retreats plus smaller workshops or classes, help us continue growing. Congregational leaders who learn together will lead more effectively.

Our goal here is to support those who are doing the heavy lifting of leading adaptive change. We don't trust to chance, instead identifying and implementing our support plan. Thereby we will avoid burnout far more often, while remaining energized for the adaptive change journey.

*Prepare leaders for principled, mission-congruent leadership when the inevitable push-back rises*
"Hey, I didn't sign-up for this." Unprepared leaders make this kind of statement when the tension starts rising in the congregation due to adaptive change. Remember the productive zone of disequilibrium? When we understand and accept that raising the temperature is necessary for mission-congruent progress, then we are prepared for push-back when it happens. We come to understand and accept resistance as part of the growth cycle.

One of the most helpful ways to prepare leaders for this is to frame the productive tension in the zone of disequilibrium as "growing pains." Congregational leaders are typically interested in growth, believing that stretching and developing are part of the Christian journey. We expect and hope for growth as we lead forward. So we connect the growth impulse with the awareness that growth involves some level of discomfort. Most of us want to avoid pain as much as possible, yet we are willing to choose experiences which include discomfort in the service of very good causes. When we believe our congregation must adapt in order to participate with God's activity in our world, then we are willing to tolerate the discomfort this brings. Recently I was with a congregation who was considering changes to their way of worshipping. They were considering including a greater variety of music in their worship, hearing from the younger people among them this musical change added meaning and joy to the worship experience. One older gentleman made the comment, "I'm not really for this change, but if it will helps open the door for my grandchildren to worship and engage our church, then I'm willing to go with it." This grandfather clearly expressed growing pains. This change produced discomfort for him (until he adjusted to the change), yet the discomfort was acceptable in light of its higher purpose.

So, we cultivate strong leadership in congregations when we equip leaders with the awareness that push-back is part of the congregational leadership experience. We come to expect this as typical, normal, and expected. With this understanding we are far more likely to continue onward, living out the principles and mission-congruent actions we previously identified, even when tension rises. In addition, we cultivate leaders through equipping ourselves with specific language and skills for responding when the push-back rises. "Yes, we are putting more budget money into music this year, and here is why." We cultivate adaptive leaders by equipping them with shared responses for when tension rises. In fact, there are times when adaptive leaders discuss whether to turn the heat up or down. Through concepts like the productive zone of disequilibrium, we are positioned to intentionally consider how much pressure to apply or how quickly to proceed. When congregational leaders can do this, then we are well-positioned to lead and sustain adaptive change.

*Ready leaders for effective team working*
How in the world do we do effective team working in congregations? Many congregational leaders are asking this question after working to build teams in churches. With volunteer leaders who rotate every year, how can we develop teams with any momentum or shared understanding?

Though challenging, effective team working is necessary to lead adaptive change. If congregational leaders are not united to a sufficient degree (not perfection), the motivating tension in the system leaks out in unhelpful ways. Team working is part of the ecosystem which contributes to the growth opportunities in congregations.

Functioning well as leadership teams in congregations can be summarized in one statement: effective congregational leaders respect team process. They are committed to the understanding that we work together to identify next steps, followed by collective commitment to communicating and facilitating those steps. The outcome of this approach means there are never minority reports or statements about unanimous decisions when communicating leadership team outcomes. Every leader respects team process.

So, how do we get there? In our meetings where we discuss next steps, everyone is invited and expected to bring their best thinking and discernment to bear. We encourage leaders to honestly and directly communicate their perspectives. We hash it out IN our meetings, staying with it until everyone is heard and understood. Then when we make decisions, everyone knows they contributed to the process. Everyone knows they helped shape the outcome. So, when we communicate the outcome and lead the next steps, we have no need to discuss which leaders were for or against this decision. We deliberate, debate, and sometimes argue IN our meetings. When we communicate outcomes of our decision-making, we are united in our communication, giving the same information. With only minimal reflection, we quickly recognize the benefits of this approach for the congregation and its leaders. We avoid sending mixed-messages while also avoiding encouraging disciples in the congregation to split their loyalties depending on who in leadership was for or against this decision. Effective congregational leaders respect team process.

*Equip leaders to reframe failure as an acceptable part of the adaptive process*
We each carry perspectives, and often baggage, when it comes to failure. Many experiences combine to form our relationship to failure. Those who lead adaptive change must be willing to release unhelpful perspectives about failure, reframing failure as part of the growth process. Thomas Edison provided us great perspective when he said he never failed to invent the light bulb. Instead he discovered numerous ways not to create the light bulb.

The central truth in adaptive change processes regarding failure is that learning and risking involves making mistakes. Those who are out there, pushing ahead and discovering new frontiers, will also discover dead ends and detours. This is part of the process for congregations who are on the move. Those who are stuck in place make few mistakes since they make so few moves. Certainly we don't prefer failing, yet we recognize that innovation includes failure. God is able to guide a moving ship easier than one moored to the dock. Adaptive leaders expect failure, reframing it as one indicator we are on the move with God.
*Equip leaders to serve as stewards of the vision*

Remember the aspirational, compelling vision? Who in the congregation is tasked with stewarding this vision? Who regularly assesses our progress, considering next steps? We need at least one specific group in our congregation who is committed to function as steward of this vision. When vision stewardship is everyone's responsibility, it becomes no one's responsibility. Too many fine visions have fallen through the cracks in the congregational system, fading away to nothing, because no one stewards the vision.

Congregational leadership teams, including the pastor and staff along with the lay leadership team ARE the stewards of the vision. This means that every meeting, the vision is part of the agenda. Every meeting we reflect on our progress toward vision implementation. How well are we moving ahead? What obstacles are we encountering? What are our next steps between now and next meeting? When there are leadership teams in the congregation who are actively tending to the vision, we all sense the movement and energy of progress. We need our congregational leaders to understand and accept their roles as stewards of this beautiful, aspirational vision.

# CULTIVATING URGENCY

*"Tell me, what is it you plan to do with your one wild and precious life?"*
Mary Oliver, The Summer Day[1]

We owe much to the Builder Generation, along with the Baby Boomers who followed them. After World War II, building the next great, stable, prosperous, and peaceful society in North America was a chief aim for many. Today we enjoy the benefits of their efforts, inheriting institutions and organizations which prospered and advanced civil society.

Yet, those who followed them did not experience World War II, nor its aftermath. Of course they are driven by different urges and goals. Mary Oliver's famous line in her poem, The Summer Day, captures the ethos of current generations. Especially living in our post-911 world, we are sensitized to the temporary and fragile nature of life. We want to engage the world around us, contributing to the common good in close-up, hands-on kinds of ways. We are those who will get our hands dirty, engaging real people up close. The desire to make a meaningful difference in tangible ways permeates our culture. Many North Americans live with a sense of urgency about making their contribution, about creating a meaningful and significant life.

So what about Church? What level of urgency drives what we do? Even more, what is the urgency about? Early in Christian history, as the Church was spreading and taking shape, the name "church" was not the only way to identify this Jesus-focused movement. The book of Acts, a collection of stories about the early church, describes the Christian Movement as "the Way." [2] People like the Apostle Paul and Felix the Governor commonly use this phrase to describe this spiritual movement focused on Jesus Christ. Many find it refreshing to reach into our history, importing this neglected descriptive phrase for our faith; the Way of the Lord or the Way of Jesus.

When we describe our faith this way we readily realize it began as a faith movement based on a way of life. Jesus described, taught, and modeled a way of living. Then Jesus called and commissioned his followers to imitate his life and teachings. We are people of the Way. When it comes to defining what the Way includes, we could write book after book trying to describe its fullness. Essentially, the Way involves giving ourselves over to Jesus as Lord, followed by embodying his teachings about a beautiful way to live and engage our world. The Christian Movement, in this sense, is more of a way of living than a religious system. When we experience the Way, we find ourselves caught up in this movement, joining Jesus Christ in the renewal and transformation of this world. It's hard to imagine anything better. This appears to be the world's best hope for a sustainable, peaceful, and just future. When we are caught up in the Way of Jesus, our urgency for involvement and engagement skyrockets.

Even so, there are some churches for whom the good news of the gospel really doesn't seem so good anymore. Perhaps they are out of touch with their need for grace. Perhaps they've heard the same old thing for so long that it's grown stale. Perhaps they don't know anyone who's desperate for love. Perhaps they've surrounded themselves with insiders so long they've forgotten how good this news is. There are many factors contributing to low engagement with the gospel in some churches. The inevitable result though is low urgency.

Before launching into this chapter too far, let's define urgency. Though we intuitively know it when healthy urgency is present or absent, a more official definition from Google's online dictionary is "importance requiring swift action." I prefer to describe urgency is with the phrase, "heightened motivation leading to action." When sufficient and healthy urgency is in our congregation, we are motivated and moving. We are engaged with God's mission and movement, leaning forward into our callings. When the reverse is true, apathy defines our collective life, resulting in lethargic movement.

At this point in the Christian mission, the early church as described in Acts provides us with two context-appropriate and relevant insights. First, their sense of urgency is obvious, dripping off every page. They endured much hardship in order to live as disciples of Jesus Christ. They encountered many forces who wanted to stamp them out. Yet each time the government or religious establishment stomped down on the Way, it was like they were jumping on a bed of hot coals, scattering them out to start new brush fires everywhere they landed. Their hopeful, passionate urgency around living and sharing the gospel was contagious.

The second insight from Acts regarding urgency is to recognize their urgency had nothing to do with institutional concerns. They were completely unconcerned about paying mortgages on buildings, keeping their financial records in order, nor perpetuating the institution. Since none of this even existed for the very early church, their urgency was not related to supporting the church as an organization. They weren't motivated to reach out to their community in order to meet their institutional concerns, attracting more people to participate, thereby contributing to their budget. Their motivation was more about engaging people around the robust invigorating Way of Jesus Christ. We will return to this issue further along in this chapter.

Evidently then, those who will experience sufficient and healthy urgency are those who have tasted of the Lord, and found that the Lord is good (Psalm 34:8). When we are captivated by Christ, we are caught up in the Way of Jesus, believing this is the world's greatest hope. We want to participate with God's mission of renewal and transformation. We have experienced the life-changing grace and presence of God and want everyone to also enjoy this opportunity. Our energy is up and we are ready to engage with God in forward movement. When we taste of the Lord, we are unwilling to keep God's goodness to ourselves.

**Institutional Concerns And Sustainable Urgency**
Often, this is the time in congregational life when urgency begins to rise. When institutional concerns are staring us down, then congregations tend to grow quickly motivated. Perhaps institutional concerns serve as the wake-up call to congregations. Maybe their purpose is to help prevent complacency and apathy. Yet, we must be cautious when embracing institutional concerns as our motivation for moving ahead in mission and ministry. Institutional concerns have a place when it comes to raising urgency, but we must vigilantly keep them in their place. Consider these insights regarding the role of institutional concerns in raising urgency.

*The fastest way to raise urgency is to encounter institutional crisis or heightened institutional concerns.* As church participation declines in North America, plenty of churches are facing challenging circumstances. Typically challenges arise from declining participation and funding levels. Though these challenges are a long time in the making, they often present themselves as immediate concerns or even crises. Terminating staff, discontinuing cherished programs, reducing contributions to the denomination, or delaying needed repairs to facilities are common examples of institutional concern management. When these challenges arise, they tend to get our attention. Depending on the level of concern or crisis, motivation for action (urgency) quickly rises. No one wants to lose who or what we cherish and value. Congregations will often rally when these concerns become the focus of their collective church experience.

*Though fast, focusing on institutional concerns as a strategy for raising urgency, is unsustainable.*
Some time ago, I served as part time Renewal Pastor with a church who greatly needed renewing. After a sever conflict, nearly half the congregation left. Over time, they did the hard work of healing followed by a period of renewal. As the Renewal Pastor, I was less worried about them in the early stages of renewal. The pain of congregational splintering was still fresh, serving to drive

urgency to rebuild themselves. My concern was what would happen when they were further down the renewal pathway, given their motivation for movement. Early on their motivation for renewal had to do with institutional survival and concern. How can we reach families with children again? How can we increase our worship attendance? How can we regain strength in our budget? These were their starting concerns. But if they stayed with these concerns over time, making progress, they would eventually run low on motivational urgency. What would happen when participation increased, their budget grew to higher levels, and they enjoyed a critical mass in the sanctuary? If institutional concerns remained their primary motivation, when those needs were met, their motivation would drop.

Though institutional concerns are helpful in jump-starting urgency, they are not sustainable motivation. The church may make progress, meeting its institutional needs, thereby reducing its urgency. But then what? The purpose of being church is not to run a great organization. Our purpose is to become disciples who join God's world transformation movement. Our institutional assets are there to help us move forward toward our purpose.

*Our institutional concerns may start us moving toward healthy, productive, sustainable urgency.* Why not just stay focused on institutional concerns as a way to motivate? This really seems to be a great strategy for poking the hibernating bear. People wake up and engage with high energy levels when we are threatened as a church. As mentioned earlier, this is a very short-sighted and short-term strategy. Also, some disciples in congregations will immediately recognize these as lag measures rather than lead measures. Institutional concerns lag behind what's really important; our spiritual vitality as disciples and our engagement with God's movement around us. As quickly as possible, we want to lead the church to shift its focus from ourselves toward God's calling. Though hard work, when churches are caught up in the Way of Jesus Christ, then their motivational urgency rises in healthy, productive, and sustainable ways. Long after our institutional needs are met, we remain motivated. Regardless of our institutional strength, we are moving forward with a sense of purpose and significance. We are captivated by Christ's presence and energizing call, moving forward with vigor. We decide we love people in our community because of God's love for them rather than what they can do for us. This is sustainable, purposeful urgency. We want the world around us to experience this healing, transforming, reconciling gospel of Jesus Christ. May we become caught up in the Way of Jesus, participating with vigor in God's reclamation project (kingdom of God) on planet earth.

**Clearing The Fields**
*"People will find a thousand ingenious ways to withhold cooperation from a process that they sincerely think is unnecessary or wrongheaded."*[3]

One of our favorite places to explore is the Smoky Mountain National Park resting along the border between Tennessee and North Carolina. This area has a rich history, including a large and extensive Cherokee population. Later Europeans discovered the natural abundance and beauty of this land, settling small farms in the region. As we hike through the back country of the Park, we often come across abandoned homesteads and farms. Inevitably there are rock fences or rock piles on these small farms. Obviously those first settler farmers spent considerable energy clearing their home sites and fields of rocks and other impediments. These rock fences and piles are enduring monuments to their work of clearing their fields for planting and harvesting.

Cultivating churches for adaptive change includes clearing the growing environment of obstacles. Every church has impediments and obstacles which interfere as it tries to move forward. Lingering effects of conflict, unresolved grief, high need for control, and struggles around power are only a few examples of obstacles to adaptation and growth. As long as these remain in the growing environment, our efforts to adapt and move forward will be constrained.

There are three effective strategies employed by church leaders when it comes to removing obstacles like these. First, allowing time to pass is one approach. Ancient wisdom like "time heals all wounds," can be helpful when clearing the fields. We can look back, recognizing some obstacles in the growing environment are no longer there simply because of time. The emotional binds resulting from those obstacles melted away over time. Time does heal some wounds.

The second strategy for removing obstacles in the growing environment requires proactive action. Engaging and experiencing new mission congruent actions removes many obstacles from the growing environment. When we experience life giving, faith-based activities with our community of faith, our previous hesitations or reluctance to move ahead diminishes. We change our minds about our church, seeing our church through the lens of hope. New experiences of being church in mission congruent ways helps us let go of our collective unhelpful baggage, becoming more open to adaptive change. Many obstacles simply melt away when we experience being church together in new robust ways. To use this strategy, church leaders need do nothing more than more robustly be who you are called to be as church, celebrating the experiences along the way. This helps confirm in our minds that we are a viable congregation, moving ahead and participating with God's mission.

The third strategy for removing obstacles in the growing environment is to directly confront, address, excavate, and otherwise remove the remaining obstacles. Time does not heal all wounds. Not all obstacles melt away in light of new experiences. Sometimes farmers must rehabilitate the soil. Sometimes the soil has become toxic, requiring contaminates to be removed. If these contaminants are not removed, new life cannot take hold.

When it comes to cultivating church and removing toxicity, we are not suggesting removing particular people. People themselves are never obstacles, though the toxicity and vitriol they carry are certainly impediments to progress. We are suggesting that some people need help laying aside their obstacles which hold them back from engaging adaptive change. Remember that a primary goal in adaptive change efforts is to ready the congregation for adaptive change. Seventy-five percent of successful adaptive change is preparation or cultivation work. In this case, good ministry with each other in congregations is helping one another remove the readiness blocks.

So, how do we know when readiness blocks are present in our congregational system, in the growing environment? How will we recognize them? Besides intuitive leaps, what indicates blocks are present? The following indicators can heighten our awareness of impediments to adaptive progress.

*There may be a block in the growing environment when leaders hear a litany of "buts" when suggesting adaptive change.* "Yes, we could make that change, BUT...." When leaders consistently hear these kinds of statements, the congregational growing environment is not ready for adaptive change. Disciples in these congregations have come to see the changes ahead of them as too difficult, unwarranted, or unnecessary. It may be they don't yet believe their church can rise up and adapt. It may be they are afraid they will lose something precious about being church together. There are many motivations for this obstacle, yet when congregational leaders hear this litany they can recognize an obstacle which needs removing.

*There may be an obstacle in the growing environment when leaders consistently hear a strong emphasis on how good things currently are.* One of the great joys of my work is to lead church staffs in learning and development experiences. I talk with the lead pastor beforehand, designing an experience with their development goals in mind. I remember two different staff development experiences wherein the lead pastor consistently described how their staff functioned so wonderfully. As we engaged learning and discussion together, these pastors were the first to speak, describing how there were no problems to be addressed. Perhaps this was so striking because we were not even focusing on problems in the learning content. The behavior of these lead pastors sent clear messages to the rest of the staff to stay on the surface and avoid mentioning anything which might be considered a problem or deficit. The urgency to learn or grow was lowered through the anxiety of these lead pastors. The same happens in congregations at large. When formal and informal leaders exaggerate or over-emphasize how wonderful this congregation is, then the urgency to adapt swiftly declines.

*There may be an obstacle in the growing environment when leaders baptize the status quo.* What we mean here is believing the way WE do church together is THE way to be church. Here's how this happens. Originally there is a reason to do what we do in a particular way. Over time, that way of functioning becomes familiar and normal to us, becoming our accepted methodology. As time goes on, meaningful spiritual and relational experiences attach themselves to that particular practice, making the practice itself a regular reminder of something dear to our hearts. Perhaps then we grow isolated from other churches, avoiding learning about different ways to do things. Conversely, perhaps we are exposed to the way other churches function, while perceive them to be somehow "less than" we are. Eventually we come to see our way of being church as THE way of being church. We give sacred meaning to particular practices, seeing them as spiritual in themselves; being the embodiment of what it looks like to be a spiritual church. When this happens, of course we will defend the status quo. When this happens, the status quo becomes an obstacle to adaptive change in the growth environment.

*There may be an obstacle in the growing environment when we see symptoms of post-traumatic church disorder.* No, this is not an actual clinical diagnostic category, at least that I'm aware of. Instead it's a way of describing the high anxiety some congregations carry when they move close to particular subjects which caused pain for them in the past. Their unresolved pain serves to heighten anxiety in the congregational emotional system. Usually this is an unconscious and therefore unspoken dynamic. Sometimes though, people will say things like, "There's no way we are ever doing that again," or "We are not touching that issue anytime soon." The continuing pain attached to this historical experience drives anxiety, interfering with adaptive progress. Whenever we adapt, we change. Changing always involves some level of tension. Churches who are skittish regarding challenging issues will likely remain relatively the same, avoiding adaptive work.

*There may be an obstacle in the growing environment when the congregation is paralyzed with anxiety due to institutional threats.* Threats to our existence as congregations do arise at various points along the way. This in itself is not an obstacle. What gets in our way is excessive anxiety over these threats. As we described earlier, institutional concerns or even crises, may jump-start our change process. Yet, we do not want to remain fixated there. To liberate ourselves, we may need to go ahead and make hard decisions, streamlining, shrinking, or "right-sizing" our budget so that we can move ahead without looming decisions. Another possible pathway is to delay addressing those threats, knowing they may recede as our congregational tide rises. Either way, excessive anxiety due to crisis or threat must be lowered through our obstacle removal work.

*There may be an obstacle in the growing environment when too many disciples become disconnected from the church.* This obstacle is tricky, since its influence can play out in many ways. What we are describing is the dynamics which arise when the critical mass of participants required to function as we do dips too low. No longer can we maintain our familiar, comfortable, and perhaps previously effective way of being church. But just like the Chinese character for crisis combines danger and opportunity, so does this particular block. The opportunity presents itself when the church grows aware that it cannot continue being church in the same way, leading to imaginative exploration and ultimately adaptive change. So, dipping below the critical mass needed to maintain our collective way of life can raise initiative towards adaptation. On the other hand, some congregations become mired in the emotional slush of grief, despair, and hopelessness. They are stuck in the danger of this crisis. This is when obstacle removal is needed. Congregational leaders can reframe the crisis as an opportunity, inviting the community of faith toward new frontiers. If not proactively addressed, losing our critical mass becomes an impediment in the growing environment.

*There may be an obstacle in the growing environment when ministries and programs are just good enough.* A ministry colleague who pastors a church who is shifting its ministry model describes their hand bell choir. This pastor and church staff are beyond the point of putting energy into cultivating this group since it's been declining for years without improvement in participation. Others outside this small group of ringers see its demise and apparent lack of viability, yet the hand bell choir itself believes it can continue onward. They are doing barely good enough to continue meeting and practicing. They can make a joyful noise to the Lord which is just good enough to include in worship occasionally. They are exerting great energy in keeping this program alive; performing extraordinary effort to keep the patient among the living. Plenty of churches are functioning this way overall in this transition time between church-as-we-have-known-it and church-as-it-is-becoming. Their ministry practice and paradigm is just alive enough, bravely carrying onward. They are reluctant to cease and desist particular ministries or programs, believing this means they are not a viable congregation anymore. The congregation's energy is tied up in keeping these programs alive, though it takes extraordinary effort, serving as obstacles in the growth environment.

*There may be an obstacle in the growing environment when grief permeates the congregational system.*
Unfortunately, many change processes recommended for congregations do not acknowledge the deep grief many long-time Christ-followers are experiencing. As meaningful ministry and program activities lose their potency, going the way of all things, this creates loss for the congregation. I'm hoping someone will publish a book on processing grief in congregations, since it's such an influential dynamic.

This description of obstacles in the growing environment is not exhaustive. We humans are adept and creative when it comes to finding reasons to remain the same, resisting adaptation. Yet, we hope this description helps your congregation recognize your particular obstacles. Naming the smaller obstacles is sometimes all that's needed in order to shrink them or eliminating them from the fields. Exercising the courage to honestly name our reality, in a context of commitment and love, frees us toward action. Simultaneously, some obstacles are so submerged below the ground that we need dynamite to excavate them from the growing environment. Naming them helps, but is only the beginning of the adaptive work. The key practices we describe next for cultivating urgency give us proactive ways to remove many of these and other unmentioned obstacles. When this still is insufficient, an obstacle removal plan may be required. A major aspect of the obstacle removal plan is to cultivate the Seven Key Cultivations of Farming Church. When these are engaged, put into motion simultaneously, the pressure increases on the change resistant obstacles. Also, the church develops the internal energy, courage, and strength needed to address their greatest obstacles as they make progress in increasing their adaptive change readiness. As progress is made toward raising urgency, leaders find the heart and strength to directly name and remove obstacles.

**Key Practices For Cultivating Urgency**
Clearing the fields will free up energy in the congregational system which was invested in maintaining obstacles. The church will breath many sighs of relief as the obstacles are cleared, noticing their energy rising. Along with this change, there are other key practices for cultivating urgency. But before launching into these key practices, this is a place to pause and consider our courage, strength, and sustainable spiritual power. Cultivating urgency is a key practice which often includes confrontation. While clearing the fields in the growing environment, the congregation comes to recognize its collective weaknesses. It's like we strategically place mirrors around the church, seeing more of who we are. Cultivating urgency includes calling attention to where we are less than God's ideal, living somewhere below our aspirational vision for being church. So while cultivating urgency, leaders don't tend to receive many warm fuzzys from the congregation. Those leaders with low ego strength or excessively high needs for affirmation may struggle with clearing the fields. This is a time to exercise our faith, trusting that God will give us the strength needed to lead effectively. Strength may come directly from God, or often God moves through the leadership cadre we have developed in our congregation. Many clergy and lay leaders connect with people outside their congregation to help them keep their farming work going; including coaches, denominational ministers, or peer groups. We don't go lightly or flippantly into the fields when cultivating urgency. This is grown-up congregational leadership work. So we need to gather all our

resources to sustain our efforts toward raising urgency. Now let's engage the key practices for cultivating urgency.

*Cultivate urgency by heightening institutional concerns*
Already we have considered the fitting role of this key practice. This is a great place to begin, but not a great place to stay for long. Yesterday I enjoyed a coaching session with Andrew, who pastors an older, slowly declining church in a part of the city which had demographically changed. I enjoy partnering with Andrew in ministry through coaching, having known him and his ministry for three years now. I've watched Andrew's mighty struggle to motivate, push, pull, or otherwise coax some life into this congregation while also trying to keep his own spiritual and emotional sanity as he leads. Many times over the three years of his serving he's given up; thinking he's unable lead them toward any kind of life or passion for much beyond existence. Now though, there is a small group who is gathering soon at the invitation of one person in that church. She grew up there and sees the need for renewal, lest this church die. She and Andrew consulted together to identify others who they are inviting to this informal gathering to discuss the church's situation.

This is where heightening the institutional concerns can be helpful. This church has practiced such strong denial for so long, they appear unaware of their downward trends and declining strength. In our coaching session, Andrew decided to reach back in time to the old but effective congregational intervention called the thirty year timeline. Andrew will construct a chart with numbers on the vertical axis and years on the horizontal axis. Three lines will appear on the chart, indicating membership, worship attendance, and financial contributions by year. These three lines will clearly demonstrate, with objective data, the institutional concerns of this church. Andrew hopes this information, along with the focused conversation led by this concerned lay person, will break through the denial enough to begin some movement.

We can see how this use of institutional concerns can serve to heighten urgency. As mentioned before, this is often how urgency begins. Institutional concerns won't motivate disciples in congregations over time, yet they can serve to jump start the process. In addition to cutting through denial and getting us started, we can return to heightening institutional concerns as a strategy of last resort. We trust that as the congregation begins moving, it will raise its eyes toward God and away from self, gaining motivation to take the good news of the gospel to its community. Then sustainable urgency is begun. At the same time, there will be slips, back-stepping, and regressing toward the unhelpful homeostasis of previous church functioning. When nothing else helps redirect the congregation, returning to institutional concerns, can be helpful. When we continue to do what we've always done, the outcomes are predictable.

*Cultivate urgency by regularly holding up the aspirational, compelling vision*
Like a multifaceted jewel which attracts our attention due to its brilliance and changing light reflections, a fitting vision draws our personal vision forward. Preachers, teachers, and leaders of all kinds in congregations have the opportunity to hold up this picture of how our world can be different when God's kingdom is enacted even more. We want to imagine together the day when the kingdom comes more fully in our community, our congregation, our personal lives. What will we see? What will be happening? This is what it means to regularly hold up the aspirational, compelling vision.

Given the primary role of the vision for motivating adaptive change, it's very clear that traditional strategic ministry plans are insufficient. We need visions of how our world will be different as a result of our participation with God's movement. By going there with our future imagining abilities, our energy, morale, and motivation rise in the present. This kind of vision is more like a video of our community when greater wholeness and peace is present. To raise urgency, regularly hold up this vision, thereby drawing our gaze and energy toward what can be. This helps motivate the church to be the church.

*Cultivate urgency by regularly describing the gap*
Sometimes we hold up the vision, inviting ourselves forward. Other times we add another action to this key practice; describing

where we currently are as a congregation. Inevitably, there is a gap between where we are and the place where God is guiding us. Our calling is to live into the gap, pushing ourselves forward like the runner at the race's end, throwing chest out and striving for the finish line with everything he/she has.

How much challenge is productive for this particular congregation at this particular time in this particular context? What does the productive zone of disequilibrium look like for this church now? Savvy leaders quickly recognize the risks involved in focusing on the gap between where we are and where we are called to go. Over time, I've discovered a guiding image which helps me visualize the leadership challenge when it comes to leading toward the gap; the creative change window. We can visualize the gap between where the church is and where God is calling us as an open window. Our role as congregational leaders is to lead the congregation into the gap. But if we push, pull, or otherwise encourage the congregation to reach too high in this window, we will risk damage. We cannot sustain the effort of a runner straining for the finish line for long. If we push too hard, then conflict, implosion or explosion, or discouragement result. It's counterproductive to aim too high for too long in this gap. On the other hand, if we drop down too low toward the window sill, the congregation is not challenged enough, sinking into apathy and business as usual. There is a sweet spot in this gap, a place where the window is open wide enough but not too wide. This is the place wherein we are challenged enough to need God's power while pushing ourselves to stretch, but so much that we go down in flames, burning out.

How do congregational leaders know where the creative change window sweet spot is at any particular time? This is when the art of congregational leadership is needed. Holy Spirit guidance, intuition, reasoning, logic, emotional intelligence, are all necessary when making these kinds of leadership decisions. We need all our skills, gifts, competencies, and wisdom to inform us about how far to open this window at this time. This is the art of congregational leadership at its best, when leaders open the creative change window, inviting us forward.

The strategy for this movement is to describe the gap between where we are and God's calling. As noted before, these may instigate hard conversations. Describing the gap is living into the role of the Old Testament prophets who described God's ideal in contrast with real time practice. The goal of this key practice is to raise urgency. So, we must lead with love as our basis, wanting this congregation to move forward in a context of God's love for them and for this world. Even when we describe ourselves as being below the sill of the creative change window, we communicate with love; not scaring people away, but inviting them forward. Boldly lead in love.

*Cultivate urgency by challenging the status quo*
Recently I facilitated a retreat for clergy who are moving to a new call. Many of them were United Methodists, being appointed to new calls at the same time given their itinerant system. Others were from other denominations who happened to be completing their current call or already engaged with a new church context. We came to the part of our day together which focused on starting well. Everyone present was highly aware of the learning curve which faces them in their first six months to a year. Time, attention, effort, and a curious attitude are required to effectively engage first year experiences while learning the culture of this new congregation. At the same time, new pastors need to lead even while learning. As we described this pastoral leadership tension, the Columbo approach was suggested. Those who are old enough may remember the Columbo television show from the 1970s. The main character was a detective who constantly appeared befuddled, asking all kinds of crazy questions. His apparent mental slowness and disorientation were his strategy for learning the truth. He used his "ignorance" to probe and learn. Using the Columbo approach is a great strategy for asking questions which function as challenges to the status quo.

New pastors can ask plenty of questions without much push back since others assume they simply don't know how things function in this congregation. Congregational leaders can adopt this approach of asking questions as a way to regularly challenge themselves and others, raising urgency. The beauty of this approach is the challenge it brings to those seeking to answer. Questions make us think, reflect, and consider. Questions stir our thinking and perspectives. Questions introduce change possibilities into congregations. Use questions designed to elicit various kinds of responses, like the following.

*Informational Questions*: "What does this church do in this circumstance?" These questions are the most benign, since they tend to focus on logistics.

*Purposeful Questions*: "Please remind me, why do we do this?" These questions invite disciples to think more deeply about the purpose of our congregational practices.

*Effectiveness Questions*: "If we were a new church, just starting, would we start this practice, activity, or action?" Rather than simply asking, "How's this working for us?" we can put an interesting spin on it with the question above.

*Missional Questions*: "How does this congregational practice contribute to God's movement in the world?" This is what we are after, so regularly asking this question helps us stay aligned with our vision.

*Cultivate urgency by holding up missionaly- congruent stories and examples of those outside our immediate congregational context*
Over time most of us grow comfortable with church-as-we-know-it. We often lose sight of other churches or other disciples who are expressing their faith in fresh ways. When leaders tell stories and describe examples of others living in mission congruent ways or being church in ways which align with our vision, then our awareness grows.

Over time, leaders learn that many people are far less motivated by logic and solid data than by inspiration and emotion. Really good mission congruent stories engage our minds (thinking), but also our hearts (feelings). This combination of head and heart when we engage stories draws us forward and increases our desire to participate. Also, this approach is one of the best ways to stimulate the holy imagination of the congregation. Many pastors now regularly integrate short videos (1-3 minutes) into their sermons to illustrate meaning, while giving brief demonstrations of spiritual insight in action. They are adapting to the way people learn and grow in our culture, making the most of available technology. Inspired and enlivened imaginations help us discover our way.

As congregational leaders use this key practice, they must be careful how they interpret and frame the stories and examples from others. Disciples in congregations who carry a dim view of their own congregation may interpret inspiring stories from elsewhere as proof their congregation is weak and ineffective. Instead of ignoring this tendency while sharing stories and examples, leaders can intentionally frame the meaning as, "…and we can too." When we observe others doing what we hope to do, then our belief in our own capacity increases. There are so many social science experiments demonstrating how watching (or hearing of) others doing an activity influences us toward doing the same activity. Engaging missionally-congruent stories from elsewhere contributes to our belief that we can also step out in faithful action.

*Cultivate urgency by avoiding the temptation to lower motivational tension in the system*
You may remember that "taking the heat" is a key practice for cultivating trust. Disciples in congregations will unconsciously test the resolve of their leaders to stay the course due to their investment in maintaining the status quo. Taking the heat involves maintaining direction when inevitable push back comes. While this is happening, there is a low level yet insistent pressure on leaders to resolve the tension introduced in the system through raising the urgency. It's like a faucet dripping in the background, always capturing a small part of our attention, nagging at us to get up and adjust the knobs so the dripping will stop.

This is when Adaptive Change Theory is so helpful to congregational leaders. Looking at the church as a spiritual farm, wherein the energy needs to be focused in the right places in order for the growing environment to produce, helps us keep the urgency contained in the ecosystem. We understand the idea behind the productive zone of disequilibrium, that the ecosystem needs enough of the sun's energy to stimulate growth. We can look through the creative change window to recognize our need for motivation to move upwards toward God's calling for us. Reminding ourselves of what we know about change through Adaptive Change Theory can strengthen our resolve, avoiding giving into the pressure to lower urgency.

When we cultivate congregations toward embracing adaptive change, there will be resistance. Make no mistake, ordained and lay leaders will be tempted to prematurely resolve the tension inherent in this change process. All our latent beliefs about church being a community of constant peace and spiritual tranquility will rise up and haunt us when we are raising urgency. The push back we receive from others in the congregation will be motivated by this belief. Our personal journeys are directly interconnected with this leadership challenge. How well we are able to tolerate productive tension, due to our life journeys and belief systems, will become clear when the push back begins.

The Old Testament prophets clearly described the tendency to lower tension in the faith community when we start feeling the heat. Jeremiah described how the Hebrew people would encourage each other to pursue peace with one another, even while taking advantage of each other. In essence, they encouraging practiced a false peace when real peace did not exist. (Jeremiah 6 and 8) Prophet Ezekiel described how the false prophets encouraged the faith community to be at peace when real peace was not present. *"Because, indeed, because they have seduced My people, saying, 'Peace!' when there is no peace..."* (Ez 13:10). Who of us in leadership has not been tempted to give in and lower productive tension? Even though it's productive, it's still tension. We want to be seen as team players, positive leaders, and empathetic Christ-followers.

Again, this is when principled leadership must guide us. This part of cultivating adaptive change, cultivating urgency, may not feel good, yet is good. Real peace, real shalom, is experienced when we are on the move with God. When we are caught up in God's transformational movement, then we experience peace

Maintaining the homeostasis, trying to never upset anyone in our congregation, slowly drains the soul right out of leaders and the congregation as a whole. When cultivating urgency, do not give in the temptation to lower motivational tension in the congregational system.

### Ripeness: Proactively Waiting For Change

> *"The kingdom of God is as if someone would scatter seed on the ground, and would sleep and rise night and day, and the seed would sprout and grow, he does not know how. The earth produces of itself, first the stalk, then the head, then the full grain in the head. But when the grain is ripe, at once he goes in with his sickle, because the harvest has come."*
>
> Mark 4:26-29

Do you remember this parable of Jesus we described way back in the Introduction? At the heart of the growth process is mystery. The farmer cultivates the growing environment over time, yet when the seed sprouts and grows, it has a life of its own. The farmer marvels at what happens.

Plenty of us who lead congregations are visionary people. We grow excited when the church begins dreaming about who and what it can become. We love to look ahead, dreaming new dreams and seeing new visions. Add to this visionary tendency the awareness that the Church must adapt to survive in our Postmodern culture and our urgency escalates even more. So for people like this, patience with the growth process which is ultimately beyond our control, is elusive. Read again the insights below which we interpreted from the parable above.

- ✓ Farmer cannot force growth
- ✓ Farmer's role in the growing process is to cultivate growing environments
- ✓ Farmers act on faith in the intrinsic growth impulse embedded in the seeds

When cultivating urgency, we want the crops to be ripe for harvesting RIGHT NOW. For many of us, our urgency levels were already extremely high before even beginning to cultivate readiness. Our challenge then is to allow the harvest to ripen before plucking it prematurely.

So, here is the frame through which we can look. Raising urgency, followed by maintaining within the congregational system the tension thereby created, IS DOING something. In fact, waiting is a necessary activity for cultivating adaptive change. When in this place of waiting, congregational leaders are not doing nothing. Their role is to keep the heat turned to a productive level, constantly monitoring urgency levels. Trust me, when emerged in this work, you will not have the time nor energy to think you are doing nothing.

## CULTIVATING DISCOVERY

In late 1803, Meriwether Lewis and William Clark led their Corps of Discovery out onto the Mississippi River, launching their epic quest for an overland route to the Pacific Ocean. Their story continues to capture our imaginations due to the magnitude and boldness of their quest. Though their story has been published many times over, in 1996 history professor Stephen E. Ambrose published his version, entitled *Undaunted Courage.* Ambrose is a master story-teller, who also happens to be an accomplished historian. This combination of high commitment to factual accuracy plus a gift for narrative story-telling made *Undaunted Courage* a joy to read. Later the Public Broadcasting System's mini-series made for television helped the story come to life with greater dimensions. [1]

I'm intrigued with their choice to name their group "The Corps Of Discovery." On the one hand, Lewis and Clark were military officers who chose men already serving in the military. Remarkably though they added other men who were non-military, yet skilled in wilderness living and survival. Though the regimented, military approach to an expedition was their approach, the purpose of this Corps was non-military. Their aim was to discover, learn, assess, relate, and otherwise engage in hopeful ways with the geography and people on the western side of this continent. They were organized and primed for discovery.

Congregations who are adaptive develop a keen curiosity for life, God, faith, and community. They are eager to engage where these intersect one another. Essentially, an adaptive congregation becomes a "Corps Of Discovery," uncovering their next adaptive move as they join God's movement in the world.

## Cultivating a Culture of Curiosity

*"I have no special talent. I am only passionately curious."*
Albert Einstein [2]

There are books on curiosity, blogs on curiosity; even a monkey named after curiosity (George). It seems curiosity is in vogue at this point in history in North America. People and organizations who learn are driven by their desire to know, called curiosity. This pushes them out the door and into the world. This drives them to open books and blogs, while engaging people and organizations in their community. Curiosity provides the motivation for exploring, questing, probing. The result is learning which we then use to adapt our approach to life. In particular, curiosity is part of the driving force within churches who effectively adapt to their contexts, growing relevant and engaging.

When doing a workshop for a denomination in 2016, I introduced the concept of "holy curiosity" as a way to describe adaptive change. By adding the word holy, I meant a kind of curiosity which is rooted in our faith, trusting God to guide our curious questing toward faithful ends. After describing and discussing holy curiosity, participants in this workshop were given the following assignment to integrate its meaning further. They were randomly assigned to small groups, given the challenge to create a video or still frame communicating this holy curiosity spiritual posture toward God and the world. No verbal words were allowed, though sounds were acceptable. These groups were constrained by a ten-minute window for planning their demonstration, mimicking life in church wherein we have to think on our feet given the fast pace of life and community engagement.

As they came to the front of the group, taking turns demonstrating this spiritual posture of holy curiosity, I found myself growing amazed. The creativity, joy, enthusiasm, and engagement of these participants were overwhelming. Obviously God has gifted the Church with great creativity and imagination.

Afterwards I found myself wondering what stifles this kind of beautiful creativity from thriving in our churches. Perhaps we have undervalued the role of curiosity. Perhaps we don't have structures and openings to encourage or engage curiosity. Perhaps we aren't overly interested in curiosity which leads to creativity.

Imagine churches who intentionally cultivate a culture of curiosity. What would this look like? Consider the following descriptors.

- Open rather than defensive postures
- Forward leaning rather than passive or neutral
- Engaging rather than fearing culture
- Asking questions rather than directing or telling

Churches that practice these postures and attitudes will learn, broadening their understandings of their world. Churches practicing holy curiosity do not posture themselves defensively with arms crossed, staring down their community. Nor do they raise their fist toward their world, positioning themselves as adversaries. Instead, they engage their world with arms wide open, inviting interaction. They are not afraid of community engagement, since they know who they are and whose they are. They are convinced God loves them completely (I John 4:18), so they know the world cannot take anything away from them. They move forward in faith, hope, and love. In so doing, they position themselves for adaptive change.

**Key Practices For Cultivating Discovery**
How do we develop a Corps of Discovery in a congregation? How does a culture of curiosity rise up and flourish in a congregational setting? Well, it doesn't happen by accident. Congregational leaders must intentionally and proactively cultivate discovery for it to take root and grow. They proactively cultivate a Corp of Discovery within the congregation. Church farmers use the following key practices to that end.

*Framing congregational calling as quest*
Stephen Ambrose describes the motivation of those men signing on to the mission; those chosen to be part of the Corps of Discovery. Some were driven by need, simply trying to make a living. Most were driven by something more, given there were less risky ways to make a living at the time. These were people whose imaginations were captured by the quest proposed by Lewis and Clark. Certainly many others believed they were crazed; dreamers without a firm grip on reality. Still others thought they were only misguided, likely to come to a bitter end. But there were those adventurers, those who were caught up in this quest to reach the Pacific Ocean by an overland route. These adventurers became the Corps of Discovery.

As long as there has been faith in God (forever), with people engaging the mysterious divine, the concept of faith as quest has been around. Journey, adventure, pilgrimage….these are common ways of describing the spiritual quest involved in engaging a life centered in God. Today's Church inherits this heritage of going on an adventure with God almighty. Christian people are familiar with these images, believing we are called to join God's movement in the world, partnering toward transformation.

When we look at the literal buildings of most churches in the United States though, we find a clear disconnect. Congregations like to own property; inhabiting buildings and putting down institutional roots in their communities. Soon after new churches are started, they quickly describe their desire to purchase land and construct a church building. Churches find themselves resembling the era in our history when God's people were Temple-based rather than Tabernacle-based. It appears that we much prefer a church anchored to the ground rather than movement-oriented.

During the Tabernacle to Temple era in our spiritual history, prophets clearly communicated that God's not so interested in permanent dwellings. Later, prophet Isaiah clearly articulates God's perspective. *"Thus says the Lord: Heaven is my throne and earth is my footstool; what is the house that you would build for me, and what is my resting place? All these things my hand has made, and so all these things are mine, says the Lord."* (Isaiah 66:1-2a) It seems God prefers living in Christ-followers as his new Temple as Paul describes in I Corinthians 6:19-20; running free in the world. God won't be constrained by bricks and mortar. Surely we know this. Surely we don't believe God is literally constrained to church buildings. Yet our attitudes and perspectives toward God and church often communicate that we prefer a God who is settled and contained in our church buildings.

To cultivate adaptive change in congregations, we must invite congregations into God's movement. It is time to reach back into our collective spiritual histories, reclaiming the call to follow. We are on a quest, discovering what it looks like to engage with God and the world. Congregational leaders can frame our calling as quest by describing quest experiences from scripture and Christian history. The Old Testament is full of movement and migrations. The New Testament continues this theme as Jesus himself travels around the countryside and through villages. The dispersion of the Christian disciples in Acts, followed by Paul's missionary travels, continues the questing-oriented movement. Questing, moving from the known to the unknown, has always been part of our faith heritage. Adaptive leaders hold up a vision of our calling as congregations as quest.

*Renewing our identity awareness, importing our DNA into the present and future*
*"The actions involved in enabling an organism to thrive in a new or challenging environment. The adaptive process is both conservative and progressive in that it enables the living system to take the best from its traditions, identity, and history into the future."*[3]

Remember this quote from the chapter on Adaptive Change Theory? When exploring and pursuing adaptive change, some congregations fear this means they will cease to exist in their current form, losing everything. They mistakenly believe that adaptive change calls for radically overhauling their congregation, becoming a congregation they are not. As the quote above makes clear, adaptive change is conservative and progressive. Certainly change is involved, yet we don't want or need to lose everything as we move ahead. This is when the conservative part of change is extremely helpful.

Every church has a history, starting somewhere at some time. In that history are signature strengths and themes. When reviewing a congregation's history, one can observe these strengths and themes as they appear repeatedly. While cultivating adaptive change, we want to conserve these good gifts, importing them into the present to further the congregation's progress.

The professional development field provides an excellent example of using identity for growth. Thirty years ago, we approached leadership skill development from the point of view that one needs to become well-rounded. Leaders would attend a workshop based on a personality inventory, learning about their strengths and weaknesses. Then the resulting training focused eighty percent of their development effort on overcoming their weaknesses or developing their less natural strengths. Since around 2000, a newer, far more effective approach is in play. We continue to use personality and leadership skill inventories, yet with a different training methodology. Now we encourage leaders to work from their natural and learned strengths as much as possible (eighty percent would be excellent) while giving small amounts of their energy to addressing their weaknesses. Our goal is not become well-rounded leaders, but to maximize our native and learned strengths. This approach tends to harvest greater results, employing the signature strengths and core identity of leaders. Rather than trying to be more like everyone else, they instead become the best selves they can. This approach raises effectiveness quickly, empowering leaders to continue growing toward greater effectiveness.

Congregations too find they are far more effective when they learn their signature strengths and gifts. These flow from the DNA inherent in the congregation. Theologically, this honors the good gifts God has given to this particular local body of Christ. When the congregation comes to know itself well, then it is positioned to adapt with integrity. Congregational leaders can invite the congregation to consider how it will express its identity now. Those who can look back in their collective histories, identifying a signature strength of Christian welcome and hospitality, are invited to consider how this strength would take shape among them now. Given their community as it currently is, how would they express their Christian hospitality now? Congregations who look back in their histories and see a willingness to work for racial reconciliation during the civil rights era are invited to consider what this strength looks like now. Congregations who look back and see their signature theme of deep Bible study and spiritual enrichment are invited to consider what form this would take to continue this strength in their current context. Congregational leaders further adaptive change by reaching back into history, importing signature strengths into the present context. We don't want to lose our identities; who we are as congregations. Instead we want to express our identities in culturally relevant ways, opening the door to the good news of the gospel for more of God's children. Congregational leaders encourage congregations to reconnect with who they are, growing curious about how to express their identity in the present.

*Raising awareness about our current context*
There is an area of our city wherein the churches from most denominations are nearly the same age. During the 1970s and 80s, this area was the suburban edge, drawing many middle and upper middle class families who wanted the suburban lifestyle for their families. This area boasted quality schools and convenient shopping. At the same time, it was not too far from the city to prevent a short commute. This area of our city flourished, as did the new churches planted in that community.

Now, forty to fifty years later, the narrative has changed. The suburbs, with their quality schools and convenient shopping, moved beyond these areas. Most of the people who populated these churches also moved further out of town. Their children are largely launched, giving them the freedom to move without interrupting school attendance. Many of them continue to drive back to these churches wherein they have invested much of their lives. They are nostalgic about these churches, remembering rich spiritual experiences with family, neighbors, and friends.

We did a major visioning project with one of these churches

There first question was whether to move or stay in their community. Through a discernment process they decided to stay, believing they are called to serve God in this community. From there, watching their process and progress was fascinating. One group in this church recognized the major adaptive change effort needed in order to engage their community as it currently is. They advocate calling another pastor whose ethnicity reflected their current community rather than only those who drive in from the suburbs. They suggested worship practices which were more resonate with the culture of their current community. They recognized their previous approach to church was designed to engage people like them rather than the people who lived in their current community. Simultaneously, there was another group in this church who believed the way they had been church was a very good way to be church. In fact, those in this community who were different than those in this church should adjust to the congregation's approach. This group believed their community should accept their way of being church, adapting to this church's culture, rather than vice-versa. This would be like going as a missionary to India, insisting the locals learn English so we could communicate the gospel in ways with which we are comfortable. Congregational denial is powerful, often derailing adaptive change. When we hold inaccurate understandings of our community context, our motivation for adaptation remains low.

To cultivate discovery, leaders can invite congregations into engagement with their current communities. Most denominations have access to demographic information which they make available to their churches. If not, Census information is publicly available.

An even more effective tool for raising awareness about current context comes in the form of living people. During one visioning process, we arranged for community leaders and public servants to address the congregation in a series of gatherings. The police chief, an elementary school principal, and real estate agent were a few who made presentations. These people tend to have their pulse on the life of a community, in touch with trends and changes in real time. The opportunity to engage live people who know of what they speak tends to quickly raise congregational awareness. Congregations who regularly cultivate their awareness of their current community context discover insights which can lead to effective adaptive moves. Church farmers encourage discovery by regularly leading their congregations in engaging their communities as they are. This realistic, present-time engagement cultivates accurate awareness, contributing to adaptive change.

*Raising awareness about adaptive congregational change*
This year I'm partnering with the United Methodist Conference in our state (South Carolina) to gather a cohort called Innovation Incubators. This is an effort to strengthen and encourage younger clergy (under 40) who may find themselves in contexts less open to change. We will gather once a month for learning, relationship building, and coaching. A primary part of the learning portion of each day will be exploration of a congregation who is stepping out of their comfort zone, engaging in adaptive moves. We believe that by telling these stories and studying these congregations, these young clergy will gain heightened awareness about adaptive change. This seems to be one of the primary ways we learn and grow, by seeing change in action. Stories and examples help us expand our viewpoints. Church farmers then share stories and examples with their congregations about the adaptive moves others are engaging. The goal is not to duplicate what they are doing. The goal is to broaden our perspectives about being church, stoking the fires of our imaginations, making room for the Holy Spirit to move among us.

Some congregations will advance their adaptive progress through making a change covenant. Remember the pressure cooker analogy? We need a holding environment which can contain the heat enough that we are safe to innovate. Some congregations strengthen their holding environment by crafting their change covenant. When the ELCA in America invests in redevelopment work with a congregation, they require a congregational vote along with a covenant for change focused on redevelopment. When intentional interim pastors are called to serve congregations, they typically make a specific covenant for what they and the congregation intend to do during the interim transition. We are suggesting that after your season of cultivation, there comes a time when collectively committing to being in a season of change is very helpful. The change covenant may include a period of time (18 months to 3 years) wherein the congregation knows they will be in a season of change. This is a way to covenant together to give ourselves permission to change, with a sense of safe structure supporting our efforts.

*Reinforce learning, discovery, and curiosity*
There's always one in the group; and sometimes two. When we are discussing issues, this one often raises questions, or points out inconvenient insights, or challenges our status quo. Prophets are rarely appreciated in the moment, since they slow the process and create more work. Yet adaptive congregations grow to where they value discovery. They learn to listen well, valuing the perspectives which challenge us, reinforcing the opportunity to adapt. Later, in the chapter on alignment, we will engage more specific ways to reinforce discovery.

## CULTIVATING ALIGNMENT

What a strange word to use while using our farming guiding metaphor, lifting up the organic nature of church. Alignment immediately takes my mind to a recent experience with our well-worn minivan. The back tires fell out of alignment resulting in a noticeable sway as we drove even on straight roads like the interstate. Finally we ordered new tires online, taking them to our local service station to be installed and aligned. Now, these new tires, along with an effective alignment, have us rolling straight again. Now if someone could just raise the cool-factor for our minivan.

Though this use of the term alignment makes sense to us, there's a better analogy involving a living organism. The human vertebrae are a fascinating and complex part of our anatomy. Though it's composed of hard matter like bone and cartilage, it's also the primary conduit of the central nervous system, sending guiding instructions to all parts of our bodies. When our skeletal system is unaligned, we go to the chiropractor or do deep yoga to adjust our vertebrae. When our backbone is aligned with our pelvis, femurs, neck, and head, then our bodies function so much better. We find ourselves sighing with relief with only a small back adjustment through stretching and popping things back into place.

So it turns out that aligning ourselves as congregations with the aspirational, compelling vision is necessary for cultivating adaptive change. This is one of the key practices which increases productive energy for mission-congruent change.

Early in my understanding of alignment, I thought it referred only to the structure of organizations. When the structure is in line with the vision, then organizations were sufficiently aligned for positive progress. Over time I've learned my first brush with alignment was an incomplete understanding. Alignment is first about positioning rather than the structure itself. The Encarta Dictionary built into my WORD program which I'm using to compose this manuscript defines alignment this way: *"the correct position or positioning of different components with respect to each other or something else, so that they perform properly."* Alignment is far more than congregational structure. Rather alignment is more about congregational functioning. When everything's aligned, then congregational flow is improved. It's about shifting everything into line with our vision. Here's an accurate description of alignment taking shape in congregational life:

> *"Alignment occurs when all aspects of congregational life are consistent with and supportive of the vision. The vision statement, the implementation plans, and words and actions of the vision community should clearly point toward the vision. But this is not enough. Alignment means that worship, small group activities, ministries and programs, budgets, decision making, organization, and attitudes of individual members all reflect the vision. Perfect alignment is never achieved. But the more aligned that the church becomes, the more effectively and quickly it will move toward God's vision."*[1]

Alignment happens when we synchronize all our activities with the vision to which God is calling us. When the farmer discerns just the right timing for planting, aligning with just the right conditions, alignment happens. When the farmer aligns the field space allotted for growing corn with the accurate selling price of corn for this season, alignment happens. Obviously then, alignment functions in congregations more like a verb than a noun. Our aim is aligning our congregation with the vision more fully each day.

## Effective Alignment Matters

What makes alignment so important anyway? Doesn't the greatest alignment work take place after adaptive change is started? To answer the second question first, yes, the heavy lifting alignment work occurs after adaptation is underway. Even so, we are cultivating the congregational growing environment toward alignment with every move in this farming church process. To answer the first question, adaptive change won't take place nor be sustained without alignment. Alignment is the process of integrating the adaptive changes into congregational life through adjusting the norms, practices, and culture of the congregation toward vision implementation. The following additional benefits heighten our awareness about the vital role of alignment in adaptive change.

*Effective alignment reduces organizational energy drag, while increasing organizational agility*
When ministries and programs are out of alignment with the vision, then we burn excessive energy administering the congregation. When the structure we are using is unaligned with the vision, then we burn energy on what seems like bureaucracy. Suppose our vision requires us to engage ministries swiftly, taking advantage of missional impulses as they arise. A congregational system without alignment, requires unnecessary maneuvering in order to implement ministry. I cannot count the number of disciples in congregations who have given up their missional impulse due to the excessive impediments to implementing through their congregation.

Agile structures remove unhelpful impediments to vision actualization, encouraging movement without excessive energy draining. Creating structures which reflect the intent of our vision facilitates movement, rather than restraining progress. Certainly there will always be some tension between missional impulse (following the Spirit's lead in the moment) and organizational process, yet we can work toward agility in our structure. We want to harvest the creative energy of disciples who are caught up in the Spirit's movement in their communities, not discouraging them.

*Effective alignment prevents and reduces conflict*
"It was not the issue itself that was the problem. It was the way it was handled." How many times have congregational leaders heard this remark? Much of what's revealed in this statement is misalignment in our systems. When our congregational systems are not aligned, then we are left with processes and procedures which do not facilitate movement. This unintentionally positions us for conflict. At the same time, our first efforts toward alignment may also raise conflict. To achieve greater alignment, we must let go of familiar and cherished activities and patterns, living into new ways of being and doing. Tension inevitably rises. Simultaneously, when we remain true to the alignment effort, we reach a new normal which is ultimately smoother and more agile. This prevents much conflict, while reducing the level of inevitable conflict.

*Effective alignment embeds adaptive change into congregational culture*
What happens when there's a pastoral move? When our leadership team rotates, how will we keep our cultivation of adaptive change going? The move to cultivate adaptive change typically starts with one person. If too many moves happen early in the cultivation period (especially if it's the primary initiator), then adaptive change cultivation stops. For this reason (and others), we want to involving more and more disciples in the cultivation process. As we move along, pursuing adaptive change eventually becomes a congregational process. As we move toward that goal, we want adaptive change concepts and practices to take root and grow in the congregational growing environment. Over time, congregational norms, values, and practices will grow to integrate adaptive change process. Alignment helps us shape these cultural factors toward the vision, including "institutionalizing" adaptive change concepts and processes. Thereby we embed adaptive change into congregational culture. Then when leadership changes occur, we avoid losing all the progress we worked so hard to achieve. We are looking for new ways of being church which are sustainable and renewable over time. Alignment lends us great aid toward achieving this goal.

## Key Practices For Cultivating Alignment

As we mentioned, the first big wave alignment work will come after launching adaptive change rather than while cultivating adaptive change. Then congregational leaders regularly tend to the work of ongoing alignment. Yet even now, during this season of readying, we engage alignment. The following are key practices for congregational leaders toward increasing alignment.

*Growing leadership capacity for alignment work*
We cultivate alignment by inviting congregational leaders into alignment-focused discussions. Early on, leaders may be uncomfortable. Many congregational leaders have not yet realized part of their role is aligning congregational practice and systems with the vision. When first realizing this is part of our calling as leaders, discomfort may rise. By starting at a very high level, we slowly invite congregational leaders into their leadership role which includes alignment work.

At the same time, remember the various outcomes described in the chapter on cultivating urgency. Some alignment takes place naturally, not requiring anything from leaders. Pain is not always involved in cultivating and implementing alignment. The importance of cultivating alignment at this point is to help congregational leaders become used to this activity. Yes, this is part of leadership; part of leading congregations effectively. Early on in this season of readying, we want to give first exposure to alignment by engaging in the least painful ways, growing accustomed to this aspect of leadership.

*Rewarding and reinforcing adaptive moves*
Every organization rewards something. Our organizational culture values certain activities and moves above others. When we are firmly planted in a consistent organizational paradigm like 20$^{th}$ century church, we tend to value slight incremental change. Safe moves, increasing organizational strength and security, are rewarded and affirmed. Engaging adaptive change turns this organizational culture upside down.

So what is it we want to reward and reinforce when we are

farming church; cultivating adaptive change?
We are looking for no less than the movement of the Holy Spirit. Adapting to the world around us, while retaining our DNA, identity, and signature strengths from our traditions, is our aim. We want to follow the Spirit's lead into the world, engaging our communities as they are. We endeavor to adapt ourselves, our organizational culture and approach, to what we and our community need in order to gather around the good news of the gospel. This means we are giving ourselves permission to be in a time of great change; adaptation. We are giving up the tendency to cling to the security of familiar practice, embracing new frontiers. We are willing to let go in order to take hold of God's unfolding providence among us. We are eager for the fresh winds of the Holy Spirit to blow us into faithful and relevant engagement with our world.

Adaptive change culture in congregations rewards movement toward change. Innovative thinking, experimental activities, out of the box endeavors, pushing our boundaries...these are the activities rewarded and reinforced in adaptive change cultures. Strategic congregational leadership decides what its calling is for this season of life and ministry, followed by training itself to reward and reinforce activities aligned with this calling. Adapting ourselves as congregations, becoming sustainable and healthy growing environments, is our goal. So we want to cultivate organizational activities and processes which reinforce that adaptation.

Now, as we describe this congregational culture change, it's clear this was not how most congregations functioned during the more stable 20$^{th}$ century. Certainly we believed we were in a season of high change then, yet we were not seeing anything like changes occurring in this 21$^{st}$ century. So during the 20$^{th}$ century congregations tended to value what advanced us one small step at a time, without radical change. Incremental change, moving the ball down the field one or two yards per carry, sufficed. Our congregational paradigms were familiar, resonating enough with our communities for sufficient returns. So, we were generally content with slow, steady progress. In that congregational cultural context, we all learned to play it safe, coloring within the lines. As we accepted that culture, things moved along fine. We learned to reinforce and reward incremental progress toward our goals. Even moderate levels of change in that context were subtly or directly discouraged.

Rewarding and reinforcing adaptive moves is the most significant key practice for cultivating alignment. We are describing initiating a major shift in congregational culture. Where we want to go is toward a culture of curiosity. We want to shape our disposition toward change into a different posture.

On the ground, reinforcing and rewarding adaptive moves looks like celebrating and affirming risk taking. We don't mean out of control risks which are unlikely to help anyone. We do mean reinforcing vision congruent risks which lead us into God's calling more fully. When we shape our culture around adaptive change, we rejoice when a disciple steps up with a new idea. The leadership of the congregation encourages said disciple to gather others around the idea, pursuing it further. Congregational leaders become encouragers for new expressions of church, rather than reluctant withholders. At the end of a year, adaptive change culture congregations celebrate how many risks for the kingdom were engaged this year. They are far less concerned about the outcome of the risk than they are interested in the spirit which empowers holy risk-taking. These leaders know that we want a culture of permission-giving, freedom, innovation, experimentation, and Holy Spirit inspired movement. So, they reward and reinforce these faith expressions as they arise.

*Embed the vision into congregational life and culture*
By now we readily recognize the necessity of identifying and embracing the aspirational, compelling vision. So many adaptive moves require the vision be in place in order to function with purpose and direction. When a vision is not in place, alignment suffers, tending toward the personal preferences of congregational leaders. Now we want to begin aligning all our activities and actions with the vision.

I'm remembering a very focused, engaged pastor I knew who made it a point to regularly ask disciples in the congregation about their mission statement. As he randomly encountered people on the church campus, he would ask, "Now what's our mission here?" After a while, disciples in that congregation learned to be ready to state their mission statement. This is one simple, yet effective way individual leaders can help us focus on our calling. There are many additional ways we can collectively train ourselves to remember, verbalize, rehearse, and focus on the vision to which God is calling us. Embedding the vision into congregational life means integrating the vision into all our activities and ministries.

*Begin assessing ministries and programs through the vision*
Later, after the change process itself is initiated, everything in the congregation is run through the alignment assessment. During this readiness season though, we begin cultivating alignment at the highest levels. We invite congregational leaders to begin evaluating and assessing our activities through the vision lens. When we look through the vision into our ministries and programs, how much do we see these ministries and programs as fitting expressions of this vision? This sounds quite easy, yet consider what congregations typically do when it comes to assessing alignment with the vision. We usually begin with our cherished ministries and programs, then find something in the vision which affirms that ministry or program. Using this approach, no ministry or program is changed because we can find something in the vision which affirms every one. We are suggesting starting with the vision itself. Remember the vision is not a high-level mission statement into which most anything will fit. Instead, the vision is an aspirational, compelling picture of how we will participate with God's movement in this world, often with particular initiatives we are engaging to move us toward that end. With this level of specificity, we can identify the relevance of ministries and programs to our vision. When a congregation assesses alignment using this approach, we consider each ministry and program through the vision. We might consider our Wednesday evening programming, for example. How much is this an expression of our vision? How much does this equip us to live the vision? How much is it worth the energy involved to help facilitate the vision? The outcome of this approach may be very different than when we cherry-pick aspects of the mission

statement or vision to support our favored ministries or programs.

*Assessing job descriptions for alignment*
When we mention job descriptions, eyes begin to roll or at least glaze over. The experience of too many congregational leaders is that we spend inordinate amounts of time on these, with little actual return for the effort. Don't job descriptions simply give us an idea of what we are about? Congregational life and ministry is so complex, we can't codify our roles in satisfying ways in job descriptions.

Given the truth in the above statement, cultivating alignment includes one major shift which pastors and church staff want addressed in job descriptions. The savvy among them want to know, "Are we working from the $20^{th}$ century church model or the $21^{st}$ century church model?" In other words, are we looking for leadership which pursues incremental, slow, methodical change or for adaptive change oriented leadership? Is this congregation looking for a Statesman (sorry about masculine language), Chaplain, and Entrepreneur...or is this congregation looking for a Faith Change Agent? Job descriptions for Faith Change Agents look very different than typical pastoral and church staff descriptions.

Just like we are moving toward a congregational culture who values innovation, we need leaders who do the same. Thus, we need to align job descriptions with our movement toward adaptive change. When it comes to annual evaluation time, everyone will thank you for this alignment move. Pastors and church staff who are leading adaptive change need to be evaluated on these efforts, not on other priorities. First and foremost, we want them to reward and reinforce adaptive moves by the congregation. Yes, this is difficult to measure, yet identify and reward adaptive work is a must for readying congregations. In the job description we might suggest the pastor and staff are called to cultivate new expressions of church, new ministries, new groups, new....whatever. Our intent is to give them congregational blessing to engage in church farming; cultivating the growing environment. We want them to grant them the blessing and freedom to function as Faith Change Agents, affirming their FCA activity. When they know this expectation is embedded in their job description and will be reinforced with their evaluation, then we are aligning pastor and staff activity with adaptive change ministry.

*Revisiting denominationally or constitutionally prescribed structure*
Many denominations are actively shifting their structures in light of this high transition time in the life of the Church. Some are specifically working to allow for more structural innovation at the local church level. The Presbyterian USA denomination has replaced the word "shall" with the word "may" in several key parts of its Book Of Order which prescribes congregational polity. Many others are working toward these ends as well. Other denominations are more congregationally-based, making decisions about their polity at the local level. These denominations can revisit their constitution and by-laws, shifting them toward more general guidelines rather than constraining documents. This work will align congregational polity more clearly with adaptive change, facilitating movement.

# **START FARMING**

Now that we know the concepts and strategy for Farming Church, there is work to be done. Now is the time for putting in our sweat equity. It's time to "make hay while the sun is shining," as they say down on the farm (at least so said my mother, who lived on a farm in her early years). Before we can celebrate the great transition of the Church, we must roll up our sleeves and begin cultivating the rich, fertile soil which is God's people. So, how do we begin?

First, remember our goal. We are Christian farmers whose calling is to cultivate the growing environment. Our goal is to cultivate readiness, positioning the congregation for engaging adaptive change. Our goal is not to initiate deep change itself, but to ready the congregation for deep, adaptive change. Even though this is our goal, you may recognize the very distinct possibility that adaptive change will occur as we are advancing the seven key cultivations. Many congregations will experience increased energy, momentum, and progress simply through cultivating the growing environment. Though our goal is not to launch the change process, mission-congruent change will organically take root and rise during the readying process. Even though initiating adaptive change is not our goal at this point, advancing the seven key cultivations is itself adaptive change in some congregations. At this point though, our primary and essential goal remains cultivating an environment of readiness.

Second, engage the Farming Church Ministry Plan. Every pastor, church staff person, and lay leader is working from their ministry plan. For plenty, this plan is unconscious and unexamined, while actively guiding their ministries nonetheless. We are encouraging congregational leaders to consider making Farming Church their intentional, approved, and embraced ministry plan. The following process describes the major moves included in the Farming Church Ministry Plan.

**Farming Church Ministry Plan**
*Discovery*
The first step in the Farming Church Ministry Plan is to enter a time of discovery; collective learning. We suggest the pastor, ministry and program staff, and lay leaders explore the concepts and practices of *Farming Church* together. At this point, no commitment to the Farming Church Process is in place. This is the discovery phase wherein those involved are learning, "trying on for fit." Here are potential ways for discovering *Farming Church* together.

- Plan a Farming Church Retreat for pastors, staff, and lay leaders; including time for processing your Readiness Indicator results
- Pastor, staff, lay leaders read *Farming Church* individually either before or after the retreat
- Make discussion of the Readiness Indicator results a major topic in a regularly scheduled meeting or called meeting specifically for that purpose
- Schedule a weekly class wherein one chapter is covered each gathering
- Read sections of the book, followed by discussions in the regularly scheduled lay leadership team meeting
- Read the entire book individually, followed by a meeting designed for harvesting the learning and discernment

Frequently we hear of congregational leaders reading and processing books together. The spiritual invigoration and stimulation they experience from collective learning is valuable faith development, team building, and morale strengthening. Some congregations will first organize a Farming Church Retreat to stimulate spiritual imaginations and gather around the concepts before reading. This approach raises the engagement level of everyone involved. The goal of this discovery step is to give everyone involved the best opportunity for learning, catching the vision for increasing readiness for change. Engaging a time of discovery positions congregational leaders for discerning if *Farming Church* will become their collective ministry plan.

What if no one besides a pastor is interested in exploring, much less using, the Farming Church Ministry Plan? Can a pastor single-handedly cultivate readiness in the congregation? Just like a single farmer can work a small parcel of land, so can a pastor use the Farming Church Ministry Plan to guide his/her ministry. Also similar to the small parcel farmer, the pastor pursuing this plan alone will see limited results. So, if no one else in a pastor's congregation is willing to get on board with Farming Church, pastors can go ahead. Cultivating readiness will benefit the congregation, with others growing curious about the progress being made as its taking place. Then others leaders will find themselves drawn into cultivating readiness for adaptive change.

*Commitment*
There comes a time when congregational leaders must choose their pathway forward. Not choosing is choosing. After the discovery phase in this Farming Church Ministry Plan, congregational leaders make collective decisions about this approach to cultivating readiness for change. We encourage leaders to make a formal commitment to God and each other; making the Seven Key Cultivations of Farming Church their ministry agenda.

In so doing, two questions will need addressing. First, to what length of time are these leaders committing themselves to the Farming Church Process? We do not suggest a specific period of time, though it's hard to imagine any congregation accomplishing this Ministry Plan in less than one year. To identity a specific time period, leaders can return to their Readiness Indicator results. Do their results indicate low, medium, or high readiness for adaptive change? Congregations with very high scores may consider a one to two year commitment. Those with low to medium scores may consider a two to three year commitment. Identifying and committing to a time period is important; functioning as part of the holding environment, contributing supportive structure to the cultivation work. When the congregation reaches the end of this time commitment, doing the Readiness Indicator again is a helpful way to assess progress.

The second question to address regarding commitment is about informing and involving the congregation. What/when will the leaders share with the congregation? What role does the congregation serve in the Farming Church Ministry Plan? Farming Church is designed to be a guide for congregational leaders. There will be some disciples in congregations who are interested and may want to read this book. Share the information as much as possible with those who are interested. On the other hand, the major role of the congregation is to engage the key practices as they are initiated by leaders. The congregation need not know the entire process with all its parts in order to participate well. Certainly leaders are not withholding regarding this Ministry Plan, sharing it along with the *Farming Church* book with whoever is interested. Simultaneously, congregational leaders do not need to burden disciples in the congregation with their detailed plan. Every congregational leader needs to be on board, yet full knowledge of this Farming Church Ministry Plan is not necessary for every disciple in the congregation to fully participate.

*Prioritizing The Seven Key Cultivations*

- Cultivating Faith
- Cultivating Trust
- Cultivating Vision
- Cultivating Leaders
- Cultivating Urgency
- Cultivating Discovery
- Cultivating Alignment

Each of these Key Cultivations works in tandem with the others. They are like the electrons whirling around the nucleus of an atom, forming an interactional dance resulting in great energy.

Each Key Cultivation is necessary to the overall functioning of the atom. Given this, every Key Cultivation is necessary and vital for increasing readiness for change. At the same time, most congregations are not able to pursue focused and intentional progress in all seven simultaneously. This is when the time commitment is helpful, providing a holding environment which indicates all the readying work does not have to happen simultaneously. The Readiness Indicator proves useful again at this point. Which Key Cultivations are your highest scores? What does this tell you? Might you first begin with your stronger Key Cultivations, adding to the strength already present? Or, might there be a glaring need in another Key Cultivation which will produce immediate returns if engaged first? Through consulting your Readiness Indicator and answering these questions, leaders are positioned to rank their priority for sequential engagement.

*Prioritizing Key Practices Within Key Cultivations*
After the previous prioritizing work, you are positioned to consider the Key Practices within each Key Cultivation. Looking to the relevant chapter, reading again the Key Practices provides the information needed to prioritize your next steps.

*Identify Leadership For Each Key Practice*
Who is the point person for each Key Practice? When we assume someone will lead an initiative, most often no one leads that initiative. After prioritizing, you are positioned to consider who is best positioned to consistently move this Key Practice forward. Considerations when selecting leadership include:

- Gift mix
- Capacity of time, energy, and availability
- Willingness
- Sense of call and/or purpose
- Fitting or appropriate team within the congregation
- Staff or lay leader driven

The goal of this step is to connect real people with real actions and initiatives. If this step is neglected, expect actions to disappear into the busy-ness of being church. Included in this step is clearly articulating the role of the pastor, staff, and lay leaders in moving this Ministry Plan ahead.

*Plan and Implement Your Next Steps*
"What's each person's action list between now and the next meeting." Are you tired of unproductive meetings? Make the time at each of your meetings wherein this Farming Church Ministry Plan is addressed to identify and commit to the next steps for each participant. Allowing each person to verbalize their next steps, with input from others, increases clarity and commitment. This also positions the next meeting to be really productive, sharing our progress or blockages since last meeting.

**For Pastors and Church Staff Farming Church**
You are in unique positions in the congregation, given this is your vocational calling and how you earn a living. Obviously, you have many parts of life centralized in your vocation as congregational leaders. To this end, we want to suggest particular practices to you as you cultivate the growing environment. Since implementing adaptive change itself can challenge us, cultivating adaptive change requires perseverance and sustained spiritual invigoration. We will need one another's support and encouragement to maintain momentum while leading effectively. Keeping our sanity and relationships in tact in the process is a priority! We suggest you consider these options for support and accountability as you lead.

- Secure a coach who understands cultivating congregations for adaptive change
- Join a coaching group; in person or online
- Find a clergy cohort or support group

Seriously investing in your support system will equip you to sustain your Faith Change Agent ministry.

**Commissioning**
"Tell us the stories again. Tell us how you helped the church as you knew it way back in the day become transformed into this beautiful faith community in which we are participating. And thank you."

There is where we are going. Because God loves us so deeply, intimately, and completely through Jesus Christ our Lord, we cannot help but love others. This love includes the Body of Christ here on earth, God's Church. Now we clearly have a role; more than that, a calling to serve in a particular way at this point in history in North America. We are Faith Change Agents. We are called to cultivate readiness, to position the Church for adaptation. We are shepherds, entrusted with Christ's Bride for safe passage toward the next season of life. Since we love our children, grandchildren, and future generations who we will never know, we accept the struggles. We are willing to endure the discomforts for their sake. We are eager for those moments wherein they will say, "Tell us the stories again." After the stories flow and the conversation moves on, we will continue to enjoy the moment, internally celebrating the journey again and again. And, there is that still small voice in the depths of our souls who says, "We did it, didn't we. Well done, thou good and faithful servant." And we will enjoy the memories all over again of when we used to be farmers....Farming Church.

# Appendix
# The Readiness Indicator

Please answer each question below regarding your congregation as it you experience it. Rate each question on a scale from 0-10.
0 = low, negative, or completely false
10 = high, positive, or completely true

## Cultivation One

| | 0 low      10 high |
|---|---|
| 1. Our congregation regularly attempts things beyond us, requiring active faith in God | 0 1 2 3 4 5 6 7 8 9 10 |
| 2. We expect each disciple in our congregation to participate in a Christian formation focused small group | 0 1 2 3 4 5 6 7 8 9 10 |
| 3. The preaching and teaching in our congregation regularly encourages us to step out of our comfort zones; trusting God | 0 1 2 3 4 5 6 7 8 9 10 |
| 4. We value and encourage the freedom to engage in theological and spiritual exploration | 0 1 2 3 4 5 6 7 8 9 10 |
| 5. We are invigorated by a strong sense of collective faith as a congregation | 0 1 2 3 4 5 6 7 8 9 10 |
| 6. We regularly engage one another in faith-oriented conversations | 0 1 2 3 4 5 6 7 8 9 10 |
| 7. We are confident God will supply all we need to accomplish God's calling for our congregation | 0 1 2 3 4 5 6 7 8 9 10 |
| Total | _____ |
| Divided by 7 to find the Average Score for Cultivation One | _____ |

## Cultivation Two

| | 0 low          10 high |
|---|---|
| 1. We give one another the benefit of the doubt when initiating change or challenging our norms | 0 1 2 3 4 5 6 7 8 9 10 |
| 2. Our congregational leaders have the best interests of this congregation as their aim | 0 1 2 3 4 5 6 7 8 9 10 |
| 3. We can count on each other to proactively resolve concerns when they arise | 0 1 2 3 4 5 6 7 8 9 10 |
| 4. We trust each other to fulfill our responsibilities in church | 0 1 2 3 4 5 6 7 8 9 10 |
| 5. When tension rises in our congregation, we are optimistic about our ability to resolve concerns | 0 1 2 3 4 5 6 7 8 9 10 |
| 6. We enjoy a high degree of trust in our congregation | 0 1 2 3 4 5 6 7 8 9 10 |
| 7. We tend to work together well in this congregation | 0 1 2 3 4 5 6 7 8 9 10 |
| Total | _____ |
| Divided by 7 to find the Average Score for Cultivation Two | _____ |

## Cultivation Three

| | 0 low          10 high |
|---|---|
| 1. I know and remember our congregation's mission statement | 0 1 2 3 4 5 6 7 8 9 10 |
| 2. Our congregation's mission and vision are aligned with God's hopes and dreams for this world | 0 1 2 3 4 5 6 7 8 9 10 |
| 3. Our congregation's vision focuses us on real people, needs, and opportunities in our community | 0 1 2 3 4 5 6 7 8 9 10 |
| 4. Our congregation's vision challenges us to become more Christ-like than we currently are | 0 1 2 3 4 5 6 7 8 9 10 |
| 5. Our congregation's vision inspires me to participate in God's world transformation effort | 0 1 2 3 4 5 6 7 8 9 10 |
| 6. Our congregation knows who it is and where it is going | 0 1 2 3 4 5 6 7 8 9 10 |
| 7. We don't invest energy in excessive or unproductive planning | 0 1 2 3 4 5 6 7 8 9 10 |

Total _____

Divided by 7 to find the
Average Score for Cultivation Three _____

## Cultivation Four

| | 0 low      10 high |
|---|---|
| 1. Our leaders regularly hold up our vision, challenging us to live into it | 0 1 2 3 4 5 6 7 8 9 10 |
| 2. Our leaders are willing to take mission-congruent risks when needed | 0 1 2 3 4 5 6 7 8 9 10 |
| 3. Our leaders are supported well by our pastor and staff | 0 1 2 3 4 5 6 7 8 9 10 |
| 4. Our pastor and staff are committed to seeing us through the changes needed in order to live out our calling as a congregation | 0 1 2 3 4 5 6 7 8 9 10 |
| 5. Sometimes our leaders challenge us to the point of discomfort | 0 1 2 3 4 5 6 7 8 9 10 |
| 6. Our leaders help our congregation adapt to our current ministry setting as needed | 0 1 2 3 4 5 6 7 8 9 10 |
| 7. We see congregational leadership as a necessary and valued part of congregational life | 0 1 2 3 4 5 6 7 8 9 10 |

Total _____

Divided by 7 to find the
Average Score for Cultivation Four _____

## Cultivation Five

|  | 0 low         10 high |
|---|---|
| 1. We know we have an important role in God's renewal of our community | 0 1 2 3 4 5 6 7 8 9 10 |
| 2. We are willing to lay aside our personal preferences about church for the sake of our mission | 0 1 2 3 4 5 6 7 8 9 10 |
| 3. We have resolved issues from our past which would otherwise hold us back from living out our calling | 0 1 2 3 4 5 6 7 8 9 10 |
| 4. We are motivated by love for God and people more than by our institutional concerns | 0 1 2 3 4 5 6 7 8 9 10 |
| 5. Our congregation has a sense of urgency about doing our part in God's kingdom | 0 1 2 3 4 5 6 7 8 9 10 |
| 6. We are more excited about the future than nostalgic for the past | 0 1 2 3 4 5 6 7 8 9 10 |
| 7. We don't worry so much about institutional concerns; focusing more on our mission | 0 1 2 3 4 5 6 7 8 9 10 |

Total _____

Divided by 7 to find the
Average Score for Cultivation Five _____

## Cultivation Six

| | 0 low          10 high |
|---|---|
| 1. Our leaders work to help us understand congregational change | 0 1 2 3 4 5 6 7 8 9 10 |
| 2. We value and encourage those among us who question why we do what we do | 0 1 2 3 4 5 6 7 8 9 10 |
| 3. We are active learners, believing we will grow and progress when we are learning | 0 1 2 3 4 5 6 7 8 9 10 |
| 4. We regularly engage experts outside our congregation in order to broaden our perspectives | 0 1 2 3 4 5 6 7 8 9 10 |
| 5. We regularly engage in learning experiences in order to stay current with church and community trends | 0 1 2 3 4 5 6 7 8 9 10 |
| 6. We are eager to discover new ways to live out our faith in this changing world | 0 1 2 3 4 5 6 7 8 9 10 |
| 7. We believe we must learn new ways for being church in this 21st century | 0 1 2 3 4 5 6 7 8 9 10 |

Total _____

Divided by 7 to find the
Average Score for Cultivation Six _____

## Cultivation Seven

| | 0 low        10 high |
|---|---|
| 1. Each team, committee, and group knows how their activity is an expression of our mission and vision | 0 1 2 3 4 5 6 7 8 9 10 |
| 2. We value changes which help us live out our calling as a congregation more effectively | 0 1 2 3 4 5 6 7 8 9 10 |
| 3. Our congregation's systems and organizational processes run smoothly and effectively | 0 1 2 3 4 5 6 7 8 9 10 |
| 4. We discontinue ministries, programs, and events which are no longer mission-congruent or viable | 0 1 2 3 4 5 6 7 8 9 10 |
| 5. If our pastor left, our congregation would continue onward with a clear sense of direction | 0 1 2 3 4 5 6 7 8 9 10 |
| 6. Our congregational activities are expressions of our mission and vision | 0 1 2 3 4 5 6 7 8 9 10 |
| 7. We expect our leaders to make organizational changes which make us more organizationally effective | 0 1 2 3 4 5 6 7 8 9 10 |

Total   _____

Divided by 7 to find the
Average Score for Cultivation Seven   _____

## Your Readiness Indicator Scores

### Average Score For Each Key Cultivation

| | |
|---|---|
| Faith - Cultivation One Average Score | |
| Trust - Cultivation Two Average Score | |
| Vision - Cultivation Three Average Score | |
| Leadership - Cultivation Four Average Score | |
| Urgency - Cultivation Five Average Score | |
| Discovery - Cultivation Six Average Score | |
| Alignment - Cultivation Seven Average Score | |
| **Readiness Indicator Score** <br> *Add Scores from above together, then divide by 7* | |

*Thank you for respecting the copyright of this published material, avoiding distributing The Readiness Indicator in other formats. We have considered publishing an online version, with increased ease of access and the ability to combine scores. If that format would be helpful and useful, please contact us so that we can consider developing an online version.*

# NOTES

Preface

1. Mark Tidsworth, *Shift: Three Big Moves For The 21st Century Church* (Columbia, SC: Pinnacle Leadership Press, 2015).

Introduction

1. Ibid.
2. John Kotter, *Leading Change* (Boston: Harvard Business School Press, 1996), p.42.
3. *"In fact, the higher the ladder the leader climbs, the less accurate his (or her) self-assessment is likely to be....Leaders have more trouble than anybody else when it comes to receiving candid feedback, particularly about how they are doing as leaders."* Daniel Goleman, Richard Boyatzis, Annie McKee, *Primal Leadership: Realizing The Power Of Emotional Intelligence* (Boston: Harvard Business School Press, 2002), p.92.

Adaptive Change Readiness

1. John Kotter, *Leading Change: Why Transformation Efforts Fail* (Boston: Harvard Business Review, March-April, 1995), p.61.
2. John Gottman and Nan Silver, The Seven Principles For Making Marriage Work (New York: Three Rivers Press, 1999).
3. Henry E. Turlington, *Broadman Bible Commentary: Mark* (Nashville: Broadman Press, 1969, p.303.
4. Henri Nouwen, *Seeds Of Hope* (New York: Image Books By Doubleday, second edition, 1997), p. 157.

Adaptive Change Theory

1. Ronald A. Heifitz, *Leadership Without Easy Answers* (Boston: Harvard Business School Press, 1994).
2. Ronald Heifitz and Mary Linsky, *Leadership On The Line* (Boston: Harvard Business School Press, 2002).
3. Ronald Heifitz, Alexander Grashow, Marty Linsky, *The Practice Of Adaptive Leadership: Tools and Tactics For Changing Your Organization And The World* (Boston: Harvard Business Review Press, 2009).
4. Ibid., Glossary, p.303.
5. Brian D. McLaren, *The Great Spiritual Migration* (New York: Convergent Books, Penguin Random House, 2016). With great

depth and insight, Brian McLaren describes sweeping changes in the Christian Movement in North America. All his books include great depth and insight. Enjoy.
6. This story floats around in clergy lore, among denominations, and among congregational trainers. While crowd sourcing its origin, I received many stories of consultants and trainers who shared this statement in presentations at conferences. One place it is found in print is: Rick Rouse and Craig Van Gelder, *A Field Guide For The Missional Congregation* (Minneapolis: Augsburg Fortress Press, 2008), p. 17. The quote in *Farming Church* is adjusted slightly to include feedback received from crowd sourcing.
7. Heifitz, Grashow, and Linsky, Glossary, p.307.
8. Ibid., Glossary, p.305.
9. The pressure cooker as a holding environment is first discussed in *The Practice Of Adaptive Leadership,* pp.29-30. In *Shift,* pp.168-70, I use the pressure cooker as an analogy for the church, exploring this far more than here.
10. Heifitz, Grashow, and Linsky, p.306.

Cultivating Faith

1. https://www.barna.com/research/americans-divided-on-the-importance-of-church/#.V-hxhLVy6FD

Cultivating Trust

1. Heifitz and Linsky, p. 26.
2. Israel Galindo, *The Hidden Lives Of Congregations* (Herndon, VA: The Alban Institute, 2004), p.143.
3. Heifitz and Linsky, p. 145.
4. Ibid., p.195.

Cultivating Vision

1. www.hatewontwinmovement.com
2. Kotter, p.79.
3. Galindo, p.183.
4. Heifitz and Linsky, p.120.

Cultivating Leadership

1. Larry Osborne, *Sticky Teams,* (Grand Rapids, MI: Zondervan, 2010), pp.102-4McLaren, *The Great Spiritual Migration.*

2. Mark Tidsworth And Ircel Harrison, *Disciple Development Coaching: Christian Formation For The 21st Century* (Macon, GA: Nurturing Faith Inc., 2013).

Cultivating Urgency

1. Mary Oliver, *The Summer Day*, poem found in *House Of Light* (Boston: Beacon Press, 1990).
2. Acts (Holy Bible) describes these disciples of Jesus Christ as people of "The Way." Find references in these passages from Acts: 9:1-2, 18:24-6, 19:8-10, 19:23, 22:4, 24:14, 24:22.
3. Kotter, p.36.

Cultivating Discovery

1. Stephen E. Ambrose, *Undaunted Courage* (New York: Simon & Schuster, 1996).
2. Albert Einstein in a letter to his biographer Carl Seelig, March 11, 1952. Cited by Alice Calaprice, ed, *The Expanded Quotable Einstein* (Princeton, NJ: Princeton University Press, 2000).
3. Heifitz, Grashow, and Linsky, p. 303.

Cultivating Alignment

1. Jim Herrington, Mike Bonem, and James H. Furr, *Leading Congregational Change: A Practical Guide For The Transformational Journey* (San Francisco: Jossey-Bass, 2000), p.87.

## *A Message From The Author*

Thank you for reading *Farming Church*. Like me, a stack of unread books is resting in your reading room, waiting for your attention. Like me, you may have a stack of books resting in your reading room or on your computer, waiting for your attention. My prayer for each book is that it will find its way into the hands of those for whom it can be helpful. I hope this prayer has been fulfilled in your reading. The trust you extend to an author, through the gift of your time, energy, and resources, is greatly appreciated. Now my prayer is that *Farming Church* will help you lead your congregation forward, joining God's love-focused movement gathered around Jesus Christ.

As you engage your Farming Church Ministry Plan, feel free to contact me and us at Pinnacle Leadership Associates. In 2008, I started Pinnacle after serving as Director of the Center For Clergy & Congregations at Palmetto Health (formerly Baptist Hospital) in Columbia, SC. Early on, Pinnacle provided consulting, coaching, and training, in that order. Over time our services shifted to training, publishing, coaching, and consulting. As the world is changing, we too are adapting. Some of our early trainings, though excellent in content, are not as relevant now. Our team is constantly searching for what can help clergy and congregations advance in our current world context. This means adaptation must be part of Pinnacle's culture.

When you contact us, we will listen to your contextually-shaped need or interest. Then we can suggest possible pathways for you to pursue. When we are skilled in what you need, we will share that with you. When we are not, we will connect you with others who can more effectively meet your need.

Currently, Pinnacle is a team of clergy and laity from many denominational backgrounds with varied skill-sets. In conversation with you, we can decide who may be most helpful to you. You may want to receive our weekly e-newsletter by indicating your interest on our website. We look forward to hearing from you and partnering with you in this wild, Christ-following journey.

*Mark Tidsworth*
803-673-3634
markt@pinnlead.com
www.pinnlead.com

Made in the USA
Middletown, DE
26 September 2017